DEAREST

★★★ A.J. ★★★

The Letters that Kept Love Alive Through the Midst of War

CHRIS MITCHELL

Dearest A.J. The Letters that Kept Love Alive Through the Midst of War

Copyright © 2022 by Chris Mitchell

Publication date: February 1, 2022

ISBN Print: 978-0-9862233-6-5
ISBN eBook: 978-0-9862233-7-2

Library of Congress Control Number: 2022901249

1. World War II Love Letters 2. Marriage 3. Children 4. Army 5. Bronze Star
6. Home
I. Mitchell, Chris II. *Dearest A.J. The Letters that Kept Love Alive Through the Midst of War*

Have Chris Mitchell speak at your live event or by videoconferencing. For information, call 972-52-438-2277 or email Chris at chrisisraeltours@gmail.com

Dearest A.J. may be purchased at special quantity discounts. Resale opportunities are available for fundraising, book clubs, churches, WW II organizations, and universities. For more information, contact Chris Mitchell.

Cover design and interior layout: Megan Leid
Publishing Consultant: Mel Cohen of Inspired Authors Press LLC
    www.inspiredauthorspress.com
Publisher: C & L Publishing LLC
Printed in the United States of America

Contents

Dedication

Dedicated to the memory of Mitch and his A.J. …
who passed on a legacy to Kevin, Brian, Jeanne, and Chris and
future generations of a life filled with "faith, family, and friends."

Exodus 12:20 (NIV)
Honor your father and your mother...

Special Word

In an age when communication is instantaneous, *Dearest A.J.* harkens back to a simpler age. A time when letters could take weeks to send and receive. A time when the words marinated in the soul, when words were chosen carefully and tenderly. When the anticipation of receiving a letter made the heart grow fonder. *Dearest A.J.* is a reminder of love stories through the ages and captures one romance out of millions of GIs of those called the "Greatest Generation." It's a reminder of timeless love that transcends our social media driven world.

Mitch's Wartime Journeys

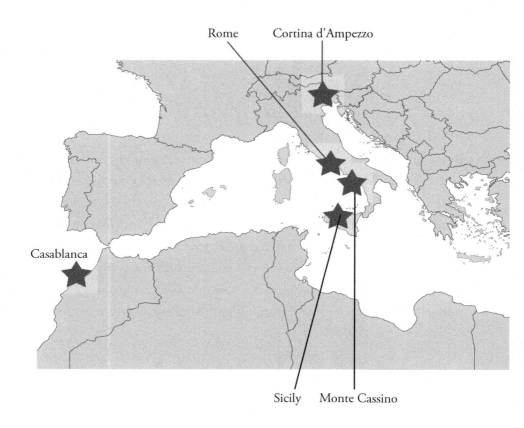

Rome   Cortina d'Ampezzo

Casablanca

Sicily   Monte Cassino

Dearest A. J.

"Arrived somewhere safely in North Africa."

The *Mariposa* that Mitch sailed from NY Harbor to Casablanca.

Dearest A. J.

"Arrived somewhere safely in North Africa."

The words echoed whispers of love from an era gone by. Seventy-seven handwritten letters and notes, hidden in the closet, stuffed in a shoe box, and locked in her heart. They held the aroma of romance, the sounds of war, and the pain of parting. Who knew she kept these treasures of her heart after all these years?

Anne Jean "A.J." Mitchell slipped into eternity on March 28, 2002. Of all the earthly belongings left behind by this wife, mother, and grandmother, the most treasured were these letters. Sylvester Chris Mitchell, lovingly known as Mitch, wrote them. He captured her heart more than 60 years before and never let go. Yet, three years earlier, she had to let him go. After 53 years of marriage and three years of courtship, a heart attack ended their life together. Death separated them last, but the war came first. These letters told their story.

As it had for millions of other young lovers, World War II tore A.J. and Mitch apart. The letters he wrote from the front lines latched their hearts together while the winds of war swept over the earth during the 1940s.

The couple's daughter Jeanne found them first in Mom's closet. Then, she showed them to her three siblings, Kevin, Brian, and Chris. These four children of Mitch and A.J. were the fruit of their love and pride of their lives.

For the four, the letters revealed a little-known but profound chapter in the lives of their Mom and Dad. Children don't always see into the romance of their parents. They also uncovered a side of Dad they never knew. They didn't know how romantic he could be, and Kevin wondered aloud, "Who is this guy?" Mitch lived his life as a loving, faithful husband, but they never knew he could be so dreamy like this:

> "… Oh! Darling how I would love to be with you, to have you in my arms, to talk and talk."

> "… For some time now, I have been just thinking, dreaming, falling to sleep with thought of getting home to you."

> "Darling I do love you so. I get a lump in my throat by just looking at your picture."

The letters themselves became a chronicle of the war and a testament of their love.

That chronicle began on April 19th, 1943. Mitch spent a few days in Bermuda before setting sail across the Atlantic when he sent his first letter. Four days earlier, he boarded the troop ship *Mariposa* in the Brooklyn Naval Yard on April 15th. This converted luxury ocean liner carried his unit, the 54th Medical Battalion. The *Mariposa* also ferried some of the now famed Tuskegee Airmen, a group of primarily African American military pilots educated at the Tuskegee Institute near Tuskegee, Alabama. Naval censors wouldn't allow him to say he was in Bermuda, but he could say he got a sunburn. He also told AJ *"The card games have been fast and furious, and I am still managing to hold my own."* Mitch likely didn't tell the whole story. Jeanne remembers a story that Mitch won a lot of those poker games. Many of the pots included tokens soldiers could use for the canteen so Mitch—a very good poker player at 29—earned the nickname "Captain Canteen."

Mitch enlisted in the Army in 1940 and was stationed at Fort Benning, Georgia, Fort Devens and Camp Edwards in Massachusetts and the North Carolina Maneuver Area. He expected to be discharged but Pearl Harbor on December 7th, 1941 shocked the world and changed Mitch's life forever. On that fateful day, Mitch, A.J., his sister Rita and her husband Woodie planned to see a Washington Redskins game but instead sat next to a radio in Washington D.C. and listened to the news of the Japanese sneak attack. They knew immediately America was at war and so were they. Woodie enlisted in the Army and headed west to the Pacific to fight the Japanese threat while Mitch headed east to face the Nazi menace. By then, Hitler's war machine had conquered large swaths of Europe, threatened Great Britain and opened an Eastern front to defeat the Soviet Union. Sixteen months after Pearl Harbor, Mitch sailed out of New York Harbor. Mitch joined part of the greatest mobilization of manpower in US history and embarked on what he would later call "the greatest adventure of my life."

Mitch's next letter on May 8th, 1943 came not from sunny Bermuda but hot and dusty North Africa. The *Mariposa* landed in Casablanca on April 24th, having survived the perilous Atlantic gauntlet. For years, German U-boats prowled the waters in "wolf packs" between the U.S., Europe and Africa to sink and destroy Allied shipping and troop ships. Ships travelled in convoys escorted by destroyers armed with depth charges to thwart this underwater terror. Mitch alluded to the danger when he wrote "one of the other companies had a lot of excitement." He purposely was vague but it's likely it was a torpedo attack. By the time Mitch disembarked, the successful Allied campaign to free North Africa from the grip of German and Italian troops, led by General George S. Patton, had just ended. But Mitch's war had just begun.

May 8, 1943

Dear Ann,

Arrived safely somewhere in North Africa. When this messed up world settles down I will be able to tell you in the fullest detail the episodes of my travels.

Our trip over was very quiet and uneventful. Although one of the other companies had a lot of excitement.

… From what I have seen of these North African Cities or in fact any of the places where I have been I am left with the feeling of appreciation that I come from the good old U.S.A. … I am writing this letter from our new camp, which is located on the side of a hill overlooking a large vineyard grove.

We just received the good news that the African campaign has come to a successful conclusion. I was in town this afternoon where I enjoyed a few beers in a beer garden located on the sidewalk. While in town I ran into some friends from my old outfit. This morning I changed all my American money into this exchange. Now I have so much paper money that I could wallpaper two large rooms. All we can buy with it is wine and beer and a few other unessentials.

How about seeing you in New York this coming week-end? I could really go for a good <u>steak</u>. But I would rather see you.

Well AJ I will close hoping I receive a letter from you soon.

Love,
Mitch

Mitch addressed the letters to Miss Anne Jean Manning, 10 Bullard St., Dorchester, Mass. (No zip codes in 1943.) He postmarked them from Lt. S.C. (Sylvester Chris) Mitchell, APO (Army Post Office) 3792, Co H, 54th Med. Bn. Mitch served in the Medical Administrative Corps. He grew up in Springfield, Mass. and came from a family of five, his older sister Peg, sisters Pat and Rita and younger brother Tom. He worked as a food chemist for Hills Brothers in Tampa, Florida and attended Ottawa University and the Universities of Massachusetts and Chicago. He graduated from Officer Candidate School at Camp Barkeley, Texas, on October 17th, 1942. Instead of testing food, he joined the 54th Medical Battalion to treat the inevitable casualties of war.

Since his first letter from North Africa, he had two months to prepare himself for the Allies' next major offensive, the invasion of Sicily. On July 10th, 1943 Mitch, along with 160,000 Allied troops, took part in Operation Husky. Forty days after the invasion, he wrote his first letter from Sicily.

Dear Ann,

"Your letter ... increased my morale greatly"

A glamour photo of A.J. before the war

Dear Ann,

"Your letter ... increased my morale greatly"

> *Aug. 19th Somewhere in Sicily*
>
> Dear Ann Jean,
>
> *Please excuse the very long delay in writing to you. This delay is in no way an indication of lapse of memory, for you have been on my mind from one night in Boston. Since I have put foot on this Island I have been so busy, only getting a few hours sleep in 24 hours that letter writing was really impossible.*
>
> *I landed on D-Day, which means the 1st day, July 10th about ten miles east of Gela. Tomorrow I will write you a long letter about my trip from North Africa.*
>
> *In my travels thru this mountainous Island I brought you a present which I will mail when I get back to the Co. I have been away from the Co. for the last few days.*
>
> *So much has happened and it is still forbidden to tell all that it makes letter writing very difficult.*
>
> *Ann I will close this short note as I am very tired for I have traveled 125 miles over these rough mountainous roads today.*

Wishing I were near you.

Love,
Mitch

What Mitch couldn't tell A.J. at the time was what happened when his unit hit the beach at a place called Gela. An LST—Landing Ship Tank—brought ashore the 379th Collecting Company, the first medical unit of the invasion and part of the 54th Medical Battalion. When Mitch landed, he found a disorganized and confused beachhead. His orders instructed him to go one way, but he saw in that direction a German counterattack. As the most senior officer in that sector, he instead directed his medical unit to another, safer part of the beach. He won a commendation for his actions but later he would say, it was just the smart thing to do, get behind the enemy.

Mitch's first letter came two days after General Patton entered Messina, Sicily, on August 17th, 1943. It marked the victory of the campaign to liberate Sicily. Mitch *"was forbidden to share"* with A.J. the harrowing physical challenges of those thirty-eight days. But sixty-four years later, Pulitzer Prize winner Rick Atkinson recounted in his 2007 book *The Day of Battle: The War in Sicily and Italy, 1943-1944*, that *"Sicily proved unforgiving. Many soldiers lost a pound a day to heat, dehydration, and intestinal miseries: Seventh Army appeared to be melting away. A chronic reluctance of cuts and bruises to heal was known simply as 'Sicilian disease.'"*[1]

Then Atkinson wrote, there was the malaria.

[1] Rick Atkinson, *The Day of Battle: The War in Sicily and Italy, 1943-1945*, (New York, Henry Holt and Company, LLC, 2007), 145,146.

"On July 23, doctors detected the first case contracted in Sicily. By early August thousands of feverish, lethargic soldiers had been struck down. Ten thousand cases would sweep through Seventh Army, and nearly twelve thousand more in Eighth Army ... All told, the 15th Army Group sustained more malaria casualties than battle wounds in Sicily."[2]

Mitch survived the campaign to win Sicily and continued his campaign to win A.J.'s heart. But like many in the Seventh Army, malaria struck Mitch too.

October 23, 1943

Dear Anne,

Just received your letter of Sept. 16, which increased my morale greatly.

Please excuse the writing as I am still in a horizontal position in bed. I was out of the hospital for five days but was forced to return when my malaria reoccurred. I am feeling fine now and am sure this present treatment will rid me of this – malaria.

I would love to be with you and prove to you that you aren't suffering from any delusions. If my letters have failed to convey that I do miss you and are constantly thinking of you I am sorry. Most of my letters are always cut and dry.

---

2   Ibid, 146.

You will notice that my APO# has been changed to 464.

(Next line deleted by censors)

While in the hospital I received your package of Yardley's soap, which is quite a rarity over here. Thanks for the package. Send some snapshots of yourself in your next letter. I would love to see the movie roll we took in New York, my sister said it was good.

Today the weather is perfect for a football game. Someday we will be able to see some good game together. Will close honey for now.

With all my love,
Mitch

Mitch spent more than a month in the hospital and went down to 120 pounds.

He wrote A.J., *"I am anxious to catch up with my outfit, my promotion should have been back by now … My day in the hospital consists of reading and playing cards. My luck at cards has been exceptionally good except for yesterday which was very unsuccessful."*

Doctors released him in late November. He survived his bout with malaria and the battle for Sicily. Next, now the war would take First Lieutenant Mitchell to Italy and into the long night of the bloody Italian campaign. His letters went on as well, as did his love for A.J.

Dearest A. J.

Somewhere in Italy...

Mitch somewhere in Italy giving gifts to Italian children

Dearest A. J.

Somewhere in Italy...

They met in South Station, Boston's busy train terminal. Along with a buddy, Mitch caught the eye of A.J. and her sister Elly at the soda fountain. They talked and exchanged phone numbers. When Mitch called a few days later to 10 Bullard Street and asked for Anne, she thought he made a mistake. Surely, he wanted to talk with Elly. Anne always thought Elly was the most beautiful of the three Manning girls, Anne, Elly and Irene. But "no" he insisted, he wanted Anne.

His attraction would grow into a crescendo of affection. But in the years to follow, A.J. and Mitch—like so many others—found themselves caught between their affair of the heart and the affairs of the world.

Mitch's letters gave a glimpse into their pre-war affair: *"the night we were at the Plaza together"*; *'Our Song'*—*"You would be so Nice to Come Home To"*—and the Army-Notre Dame football game. For many Irish Americans, Notre Dame University—the largest Catholic college in America—played a big part in Mitch and Anne's life. First generation Irish Americans, their families left Ireland in the early 1900's to start a new life in America. Anne's mother came from County Mayo and her dad from County Galway. Mitch's mom and dad both came from County Kerry where the saying went, "the next parish is Boston." Mitch loved Notre Dame football and in the 1940s he had a lot to cheer about. From 1940 to 1949, they were the gold standard of college football in America. They won national championships in

1943, 1946, 1947 and 1949 and had six undefeated seasons. But by the fall of 1943, the affairs of the world had intervened and for the first time in five years, Mitch missed the Army-Notre Dame game. Instead, Mitch left his hospital bed in Sicily, joined up with his unit "somewhere in Italy" and became part of the Fifth's Army advance up the Italian peninsula.

Nov. 21, 1943

Dearest A.J., Somewhere in Italy

Just caught up with my outfit yesterday. I found seven of your letters waiting for me and your package. Your letters were dated from Sept. 7th to Nov. 8th. Thanks a lot hone. I will try to answer one of your letters each day – so here goes for your Sept 7 letter – first I will take time out to read it again (fifth time). By the way, I am feeling O.K.

I liked the paragraph in which you said how much you missed me. That is the way I want you to feel, but I hope we both don't have to feel that way too long, this mess will end soon. Lets hope and pray it will.

You mentioned the night we were at the Plaza together. What I wouldn't give to be back there with you right now. It was snowing that night but it was a good snow.

Honey send a few snap shots of yourself, if you don't have any have some taken. Have them about the size that would fit inside a cigarette case – that could be carried with me.

I flew over from Sicily – someday soon I hope I will be able to tell you about the trip.

I feel bad about not being able to send you something nice for Xmas. I should find something nice in Italy to send you.

Will close honey until tomorrow.

All yours,

Love
Mitch

A.J. greeted Mitch with seven letters, but we don't have those letters and the many more she wrote during the war. Her side of their wartime love story is now reflected through Mitch's replies. We do know A.J.'s letters, like millions of other women's letters, inspired their men. One woman described how to write a letter to men at war: "Soldiers are occupied with the fundamentals of existence. Yours, as well as theirs, only most of you are too far away from the terribleness of war and what a Nazi-dominated world could mean, to realize it. Yes, I know. It's very hard to suddenly become a psychologist and an author overnight merely because your man went away. But it's worth your while to try. For just as the right kind of letters will tighten your romances —or your bonds of affection with son, brother, or husband —so will the wrong kind loosen them".[3]

---

3   Rosemary Ames, "Sabotage Women of America"; File E-NC-148-57/181; OWI Intelligence Digests, Office of War Information, Record Group 208; National Archives at College Park, Maryland; 4-5.

A.J. attended the Katharine Gibbs Secretarial school in Boston. During the war, A.J. worked for her father, Michael Manning. He owned a limousine company in Boston and hired out drivers and cars for weddings, funerals, and other occasions. Her heart would jump when Mitch's letters arrived at Bullard Street. Years later, she told her kids, "I'd be at work and my mother would say 'there's something here for you, 'V-mail' and I would say to my father, I'll be right back. And I'd rush home."

Mitch's letters often came as V-mail. V-mail (Victory-mail) was the U.S. Army's solution to the enormous volume of mail during the war. To save on bulk and weight, they micro-filmed the letters and sent them instead of the original. During the course of the war, more than a billion V-mails – including Mitch's went back and forth overseas.

But there were limits to what he could say. A.J. once told her kids, "He told as much as he could in the V-mail, but he had to be careful. Everything was censored in and out of the country. You had to be very casual in what you were saying." One asked, "They didn't read everything did they?" A.J. answered, "Oh you better believe it. They had to when the war was on. He couldn't be too explicit."

In November 1943, Mitch couldn't tell A.J. his unit—the 54th Medical Battalion—was officially part of the Naples-Foggia Campaign. It began Sept. 9th. Before the war's end, Mitch and the 54th would see action in three more campaigns, the Rome-Arno, the North Apennines, and the Po Valley. By the time Mitch arrived after his bout with malaria in Sicily, ferocious fighting already marked this first campaign. The Fifth Army met stiff German resistance. There would be much more opposition. Hitler poured men and machine into Italy to stop the Allied advance.

Dec. 3, 1943

Dear Anne, Somewhere in Italy

... it is now 7 o'clock and off in the distance the artillery can be heard. They are really laying it on. You get so accustomed to the noise that when it stops you feel a little uneasy...

Well my sweet one I will close until tomorrow.

All yours,
Mitch

Along with the artillery came Christmas and thoughts of home.

Dec. 24, 1943

Dearest A.J.,

I received your letter containing the snapshots. One of which I cut down to fit my cigarette case, so everytime I have a cigarette I must first take a look at you. As of yet I haven't received the large picture; it may be in the mail tonight (the mail clerk just left – I told him not to come back without a letter from you).

I just finished censoring some of the Company mail and by their letters the men are a little homesick. It is tough to spend Xmas here with artillery in lieu of sleigh bells, but it could be much worse. First we should be thankful to be alive and well, and we are much better off than most of the Italian people whose homes and towns are left in a pile of debris by war.

Honey I am a little homesick and hope and pray that next Xmas I will be home and with you.

Did you receive the package I sent you? I hope you like the gloves.

Well Honey I will close this short note and will write tomorrow.

All my love,
Mitch

December 25th, 1943 marked their first Christmas apart, and a long way from the little town of Bethlehem.

Dearest A.J.

I have been thinking about you most of the day. What you are doing etc. I hope your Xmas was a pleasant and happy one.

Today we had a wonderful Xmas dinner. It is unbelievable what can be done in the field a few miles behind the lines. We sat down to a table with a clean white linen tablecloth. The menu consisted of roast turkey, which was delicious, mashed potatoes, mashed sweet potatoes, peas and carrots, dressing, giblet gravy, white and raisin bread, fresh butter, fresh fruit, oranges, apples, and almond nuts, wonderful cherry and raisin pies, cookies formed in stars, Xmas trees and crosses, coffee and wine. What do you think of that for a menu? Oh yes we had the echo of artillery for music.

On a clear day, which is seldom, the scenery is beautiful. High with capped mountain ranges and deep green fertile valleys. But the weather spoils all its beauty, rain day after day.

Everyone in the company except the guards have gone to bed so I will join the rest and jump into my sleeping bag and dream of Boston or 10 Bullard St.

Goodnight my sweet one,

Love,
Mitch

But Mitch's dreams of 10 Bullard Street and A.J. would have to wait. They both looked forward to 1944 with hope but would soon discover it would be the hardest year of all.

Deaust A. J.

"At present it is rather difficult to write..."

US troops heading up to the next battle in the Italian campaign

https://catalog.archives.gov/id/531277

Dearest A. J.

"At present it is rather difficult to write…"

1943 ended with a dream. 1944 began with a prayer.

January 9, 1944

Dear A.J.,

"…I hope and pray that this mess will be over soon. I have seen all I want to see. The U.S. will really look good to me, so will you. Won't we do the rounds the day I get my feet on that precious soil? You know dear the people in the U.S. don't know how lucky they are.

Honey I hope my letters don't sound or read depressing.

Hope all is well.

I love you

Love,
Mitch

On January 14, 1944, Mitch wrote A.J.: "Honey please excuse these short and irregular letters. At present it is rather difficult to write."

At the start of 1944, the Allies were preparing for Operation Overlord, the historic landing on the beaches of Normandy that would change the course of history six months later, on June 6th, 1944. Operation Overlord would shorten the war, but it also drained men and materiel from other fronts including the Italian campaign, sometimes known as the "Forgotten Front." But through the winter of 1944, the men of Fifth Army, including Mitch, endured mud, cold and exhaustion, to steadily advance up the Italian countryside.

It was difficult. Mitch and the Fifth Army faced the ferocious resistance of the German army commanded by Field Marshall Albert Kesselring. The combination of battle-hardened German soldiers, man-made defenses and natural barriers made the Italian front one of the most formidable battle fields of World War II. The Allies faced German defensive lines called the Volturno, the Barbara, and the Gustav.

Mitch's 379th Medical Collecting Company – part of the 54th Battalion—followed the Fifth Army's advance. They trailed some of history's greatest war machines ever assembled, battle groups that faced off in mortal combat. The "379th" collected the human debris of war. Mitch often told A.J. he was "busy" but didn't explain. Mitch was busy with the grim business of war. He set up field hospitals just behind the front lines. He directed combat ambulances. He made triage calls, the life-and-death decisions of who needed medical attention immediately, who could wait, and who was beyond help. This was the gruesome business of war Mitch lived in 1944.

Even if he could, he wouldn't tell A.J. what this business looked like from day to day. But Atkinson again in *The Day of Battle* shares how the famous war correspondent Ernie Pyle described a typical field hospital: "Nearly a week in a field hospital brought more awful visions. 'Dying men were brought into our tent, men whose death rattle silenced the conversation and made all of us thoughtful,' Pyle wrote. A trench outside a surgical tent was 'filled with bloody shirt sleeves and pant legs the surgeons had snipped off wounded men.' Pyle noted 'how dirt and exhaustion reduce human faces to such a common denominator. Everybody they carried in looked alike.'"[4]

---

4   Atkinson, 146.

After the war, Mitch would tell how much he admired the surgeons.

Atkinson paid them tribute too.

"The unlucky relied on the heroic efforts of doctors and nurses working in dreadful conditions. Surgeons operated by flashlight, with white sheets hung in the operatory for more reflected light. After watching surgeons lop off limbs for an hour, Frank Gervasi, a reporter for Collier's magazine, recalled Erasmus's astringent epigram 'Dulce bellum inexpertis': Sweet is war who have never experienced it.'"[5]

Mitch often worked under fire. He particularly hated artillery. After the war, he described what it was like to be under bombardment. "You knew you couldn't do anything about it but just dig your own hole and do a lot of praying."

It's said there are no atheists in foxholes, but Mitch entered his foxhole with faith and a prayer. After the war, he said he would pray the prayer of Saint Andrew when he didn't think he would make it:

"Hail and blessed is the hour and moment in which the Son of God was born of the most pure virgin in Bethlehem at midnight in the piercing cold. In that hour vouchsafe oh my God to hear my prayers and grant my desires through the merits of the Son of God and his virgin Mother Mary."

He told A.J. it was "sweating them out."

Feb. 18, 1944

Dearest A.J.

"... I had a good time at the Officers Rest Center, but it was impossible to rest when you knew you were on

---

5   Atkinson, 145.

borrowed time and that in a few days you would be back
'sweating them out' (waiting for the shells to come in)."

Mitch would say after the war one learned the sound of incoming German shells and the outgoing American salvos. Perhaps only those who have been under artillery bombardment know its sheer terror. One time Mitch recounted the experience of "sweating them out" and reliving the experience became so real he began to sob.

February 1944 was a hard month for Mitch. Valentine's Day came and went without Mitch sending out a Valentine. Instead, he witnessed one of the most controversial decisions of World War II, the bombing of Monte Cassino. This 6th century monastery stood atop one of the most strategic mountains blocking the Allied advance and the road to Rome. After weeks of debate, Allied planes dropped more than one thousand tons of bombs on the most important monastery in Europe and reduced it to rubble. After the war, Mitch praised the many fighters who finally captured the strategic heights, especially the Polish soldiers. They went behind the lines by climbing over the mountain passes and, in the process, suffered great losses and casualties. Their cemetery is the highest on Monte Cassino to this day.

Mitch was there to see it. On April 6, 1944 he told A.J.: "... In your letter you mentioned seeing pictures of the bombing atop Mt Cassino. I would like to see those pictures as I had a bird's eye view of the same. That should answer your question."

Dearest A. J.

"Sitting by a fire...

reading some of your letters"

A.J. outside home at 10 Bullard Street, Dorchester, MA

"Sitting by a fire... reading some of your letters."

Still, near the front lines and *"sitting by a fire"* his thoughts were never far from A.J.

Feb. 22, 1944

Dearest A.J.

"I have been sitting by a fire for the last fifteen minutes reading some of your letters, which I have been saving. Just finished reading the letter where you mentioned receiving the cameos. I am glad you liked them. I am sure they will look nice on you – you cute thing. I think of you constantly and long for the day of our reunion. Many times have I thought how nice it would be to be able to go to the phone and say honey, 'how about meeting me in New York?' Or to be dancing with you at the Plaza.

"... The mail just came in and I received your Valentine. Honey I was unable to send one, but you are my Valentine —with all my heart."

From one who cares.

All my love,
Mitch

In early 1944, Mitch experienced one of war's unexpected twists. His younger brother Tom—a new replacement—got assigned to a nearby unit in Italy. He was a "ninety-day wonder"—those recruits who trained for three months and then sent over to replace the dead or wounded.

He began telling A.J. the story.

April 6, 1944

"From my last letter from home I learned that my brother is on his way over here. I feel sorry for him, as it is tough for Inf. Replacements. They get tossed around from replacement pool to replacement pool and are green when they do hit a permanent outfit, which is usually on the line."

April 15th, 1944 *"I met him (Tom) yesterday here in Italy. I feel for him because he is a replacement depot and infantry at that. Tomorrow I am going to spend the whole day with him."*

April 22, 1944 *"Yesterday I saw my brother for the second time. He is fine, but right now is in a Replacement Pool, which is like being a little stone on a beach waiting for someone to pick you up ... I am trying to get him into the Bn. (Battalion). I hope I am successful."*

Two days later, Mitch told A.J.

"Since I started this letter my brother has been assigned to the Bn. Isn't that a break? I thank God that I was in a position to help him out. Later I hope to get him into the Finance Dept. where he can put his training to good use both for him and the Army."

Tom didn't get to the Finance Dept. but instead made it in Mitch's 379th Medical Battalion. When Mitch finally got permission to have Tom re-assigned to the 379th he went to Tom's unit with his transfer orders. When he asked for Thomas Mitchell, a forty-year-old man showed up and Mitch said, "You're not Thomas Mitchell!" They sent the wrong "Thomas Mitchell" but soon the real Thomas Mitchell showed up. When Tom asked Mitch what he should do with his rifle, Mitch said put it over there next to a tree. Soon Tom and Mitch drove back to the 379th where Tom traded his gun for a litter. Mitch always thought it saved his life though both saw the bitter side of war. None of the men in Tom's original unit ever came home.

Years later, Peg—Mitch's sister—told some of their own war stories.

Peg remembered, "One thing that was good for us, the nurse's unit that was attached to their unit had a nurse in it that was a sister of Mitch's best friend, Louise Derico. She used to write home every day to her mother and father. And her sister would call us up because in her letter she would always mention Chris. How he was doing and where he was."

"The only story (Tom) told was. They laid down wires for communication and he and another guy went out there. They were following the wires and seeing them once and a while. But Tom was color blind, and they didn't know that the wires they were picking up were German wires. The two of them were walking unknowingly into a German encampment. Finally, they decided they were too far away from their own lines and they'd better turn back. When they got back, they found out they had been in the German area."

By 1944, the war effort demanded fresh troops like Tom. The replacements came over 'green' and ill trained. Mitch almost suffered the consequences. Peg said, "One man shot at Mitch. He had never seen a medical officer dressed in all the things he carried for safety and he thought (Mitch) was a German and shot at him but he missed."

Another story exemplified the fog of war: "There was quite a big battle and the Americans were losing … a German plane went over and dropped a bomb and it fell between the unit where your father was and where Tom (Mitch's brother) was. And each one thought the other's unit got hit and your father took us to that spot where the bomb fell."

Peg also recalled, "We were scared to death, my Mother and I. Sure, your father was in the fighting and in the action. He was up front." "Mitch brought home a Bible that (another soldier) had worn on his chest. The Bible had a metal back on it. It saved the guy's life."

After the war, Mitch described his own personal brush with death and one of his greatest personal losses of the war. He and three other soldiers from his medical company were near the front. Suddenly they came under German mortar fire and took cover in a nearby church. With shells landing close by, Mitch's driver found himself on one side of the church with the others on the other side. He thought that where the other guys were was safer so he raced over and past an open window. A piece of shrapnel hit him in the throat. He died before hitting the ground. It's was Mitch's closest personal loss of the war.

Mitch's letters to A.J. left many things about his wartime experiences untold. Pen and paper never recorded the scenes he and Tom undoubtedly witnessed. As a litter bearer, Tom picked up the dead and wounded. Munitions do not injure, maim, and kill cleanly or quietly. He did not mention the screams for "Medic" or "Mama." He did not tell of the gruesome wounds too horrible to tell or pain so deep even morphine couldn't reach. These are the sounds and sights seldom spoken by the men of war. A.J. once said, "He never told us all the stories." Peg added, "Neither did Tom."

Despite the horrors of war, Mitch poured out a constant theme in his letters ... his longing and love for A.J.

April 22, 1944

Dearest A.J.

"... I write so little. In fact I started to write this letter two days ago, but just couldn't get to it. Honey don't judge my love to the amount of letters I write you. If you did I would have to be writing all the time."

Dearest A. J.

"... that was the night I knew ..."

A.J.'s glamour photo

Dearest A. J.

"... that was the night I knew ..."

During those difficult days of 1944, Mitch mentioned two special rendezvous in New York City.

April 15, 1944

"... Do you remember the night we parted in the Penn. Sta ... that was the night I knew."

May 19, 1944

Dearest A.J.

"... I was very sure I loved you when tears came to my eyes when I left you at the Grand Central Station. Do you remember? ... Darling it shouldn't be too long before we are together again. Let's both pray that the time will be short and pass fast.

I am in good health – no pain except a big spot in my heart."

All my love,
Mitch

And he dreamed of their next rendezvous.

June 15, 1944

Dearest A.J.

"...For sometime now I have been just thinking, dreaming, falling to sleep with thoughts of getting home

to you. How you will look — How I will look to you —
What we will do —What we will say to each other when
we first meet. Have you any plans as to where we should
meet and what we should do on that wonderful day? I
think of you so much, but I never seem to be able to really
put my thoughts on paper. ... Your letter of March 28th
was wonderful. I have read and re-read it many times. It
has been over a year since we have seen each other and I
miss you more each hour — I am glad you are suffering
with me. ... Hoping you are well my precious one, I will
close with all my love."

Mitch

In June, Mitch witnessed one of the great triumphs of the Italian campaign, the liberation of Rome. The Allies succeeded in doing something only one other army in history had accomplished, capturing the Eternal City from the south. It wasn't easy. The Commander in Chief of Allied forces in Italy British General Harold Alexander quipped, "All roads lead to Rome, but all the roads are mined." Still, Allied forces drove on and entered Rome on June 4th, 1944. Mitch was there with A.J. on his heart.

June 15, 1944

"The ring I sent you was bought in Rome, the first day
the city fell to the Allies. It may not fit your finger and
it will not compare to the rock your Dad gave you, but
I had to buy something that memorable day ... Rome is
a very beautiful city comparable and in some ways nice

as our cities ... St. Peter's Cathedral is so beautiful and filled with priceless art and historical treasures, that one could spend days visiting it ... The country around Rome is very beautiful with fields and rolling hills just covered with poppies and other flowers. I would give anything to have you with me, seeing these things with this war not in existence. Here and there the effects of war spoil the natural beauty, a bridge blown up, a tank knocked out, a field burnt and full of shell holes ... "

Two days after Rome fell, Allied forces landed on the beaches of Normandy. "Humanity's beachhead" spelled the beginning of the end of the Nazi grip on Europe. Mitch shared the good news with A.J.

June 9, 1944

Dearest A.J.,

"... What did you think of the Invasion News? We were thrilled here especially when it came at the same time as the fall of Rome. I hope and pray that it is successful and that this mess will be over with very little bloodshed.

This morning I sent you a ring as a souvenir of a great city. I hope you like it. All my love goes with it.

I could write so much but censorship wouldn't approve ... Well darling will close with all my love. Hoping you are well.

Write often
Love, Mitch

He rejoiced in their victories. But a tenacious enemy and a maddening war continued to keep Mitch away from his A.J.

July 26, 1944

Dearest A.J.

"…It looks like this — war will be over soon, at least the end is in sight. The Germans still have a lot of fight left in them even they know they lost the war. It looks like they are intent on making it a costly victory.

Darling everyday that passes is a day nearer to home and a day closer to you. Let's hope and pray that God will hasten the end.

Will write tomorrow.

All my love,
Mitch

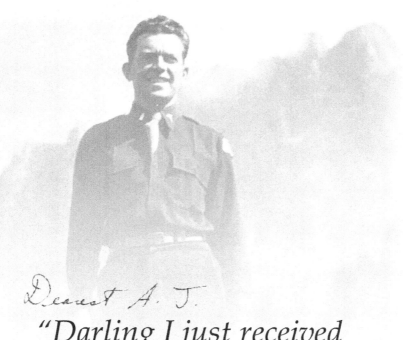

Dearest A. J.

"Darling I just received your Valentine..."

Mitch standing outside Cortina d'Ampezzo

Dearest A. J.

"Darling I just received your Valentine…"

Throughout the summer and the long fall of 1944, Mitch slogged through the bitter Italian campaign. On 10 Bullard Street, A.J. fought the battle on the home front of rations and deprivation for the war effort. But they both faced the timeless battle fought by lovers throughout the ages—uncertainty—born of time, distance, and doubt.

Months after the fall of Rome, Mitch felt the need to let A.J. know that no woman could take her place. As the director of field hospitals, he worked closely with both doctors and nurses. His letter on October 6th, let A.J. know they were no match for her:

Oct. 6, 1944

Dearest A.J.

Just received your letter of Sept. 8, and how I would have loved to have been there sitting with you against the sea wall. What a difference in atmosphere. I am writing this letter in one of the worst storms we have had this year by candlelight. It is raining, thundering, and lightening, and I expect this tent to go down soon. We are fortunate though – as we have acquired a nice stove, which keeps us warm and dry. I am glad I don't have to go out tonight – my heart goes out to those Infantry soldiers out there in holes filled with water. The mud in these mountains is knee deep. Even in this tent the mud is ankle deep and the stove has been going continually for three days. Enough of my complaints.

Listen my sweet one what gave you the idea I was coming home with a nurse? Let me get you straight on this matter. I do know a few nurses, but none well enough to take home, nor any that I want to take home. I haven't seen anything in my travels that I want to take home. Since I met you there has been nobody but you. I hope you are straight on this subject. You better be or your little ears will get the cutting instead of my big ones. Don't worry about the nurses honey we are seldom very near them, occasionally we are set up near a field hospital, but usually we are quite a few miles in front of them. Even if they were with us there isn't any of them that can get you off my mind..."

"Darling I have but one wish and that is to get back on the other side of the pond to you and the sea wall. How about throwing me a rope?

My sweet I will close this letter, as the wind is coming up again, and the candle is about to blow out.

All my love,
Mitch

While Mitch fought the battle of keeping his love true on the front lines, A.J. fought her own battle back home. Jeanne tells the story of

John Phelan, an Army pilot who flew all the way from Texas to Boston to see A.J. She rebuffed the offer. It was through these uncertain times, that their letters held these two lovers together ... and their faith.

Dec. 26, 1944

Dearest A.J.

"Darling it has been a long time since we have been separated. But as you say God is good, he will bring us together soon again."

By the end of 1944, Mitch and A.J. suffered through their second Thanksgiving, Christmas, and New Years apart. Mitch poured his heart out in his words and in his prayers.

Jan. 4, 1945

Dearest A.J.

"...Your Xmas card was wonderful. I still put it under my head when I go to bed. Really darling I don't know what I would do without you. You are what keeps my spirit going thru all this mess. All I want is to get home to you. I have never had anyone mean so much to me. Gee darling I am praying my heart out, but I am very lonely for you ..."

From one lonely heart to another, Mitch sent A.J. his Valentine's Day Card of 1945:

A VALENTINE
From One who Cares

You'll never know how much I care –
How much I think about you –
Words cannot tell you how I feel,
So far away, without You –
But meanwhile, all my thoughts are in
This Valentine I'm sending –
A world of love, and wishes, too,
For happiness unending!

All my love,
Mitch

Mitch continued to pour out his heart.

Feb. 21, 1945

Dearest A.J.

"Let me start off by telling you how much I miss you, and how I long for the day we are together again. Darling I do love you so. I get a lump in my throat by just looking at your picture. Darling I do want to get home soon. I am so sick of this war, but it looks like the end is in sight – I hope so."

"In your letter of Jan.26 you mentioned having attended a wedding in which there was no head or tail to it. What kind of a wedding do you want my sweet? Or should we

wait until I get home so you can tell me. It will be much nicer to talk about than to write about.

Darling you don't have to fear about the nurses and WACS over here even if they were Hollywood's best. Your are all that I want.

I will never forget how I felt that night I left you on the train in the Grand Central Station. It was then that I was sure, oh so sure, that I had it bad … "

All my love,
Mitch (or Ves)

Then Mitch received A.J.'s Valentine.

Feb. 24, 1945

Dearest A.J.

Darling I just received your Valentine, which I had been waiting for. It was very nice.

This is Saturday night and always the loneliest night of the week for me. Oh! Darling how I would love to be with you, to have you in my arms, to talk and talk. I wonder what you are doing tonight. I sit and brood over how we are cheated of so many precious moments on account of this terrible war. I am not complaining darling. I also get a lot of enjoyment dreaming about you and the things we will do when I return.

War news is again looking good. Although the end is in sight the war will be as hard or even harder than before. Everyone over here has given up predicting the date of its end, but hoping it will be over soon.

Will close darling hoping all is well with you, and that you are thinking of me tonight.

All my love for you,

Mitch

"This terrible war" as Mitch called it was "as hard or even harder than before." Battles fought for months from the next ridge to the next mountain to the next valley left the men and machine of the Fifth Army weary and exhausted. They still faced a highly skilled and stubborn foe. Yet as the winter of 1944 turned into the spring of 1945, the Fifth Army stood on the cusp of its final advance of the war. Up north, American troops crossed the Rhine River onto German soil on March 7th, 1945. In Italy, the North Apennines campaign pushed the Germans past the vaunted Gothic Line and the Allies prepared for the campaign towards the Po Valley. By Valentine's Day 1945, the world may still have been at war, but spring and the scent of the war's end was in the air. Mitch hoped—and prayed—one day soon he and A.J. would be together.

Dearest A. J.

"... The war news is wonderful. It should be over soon."

Mitch and A.J. outside St. Peter's just after their wedding

61

Dearest A. J.

"… The war news is wonderful. It should be over soon."

In the spring of 1945, the Fifth Army amassed more than a quarter of a million men for its final push north. It was the beginning of the end. Mitch could feel it.

March 28, 1945

> *"Your letter was wonderful. Oh! Anne it did so much for me. The men know that they can ask for almost anything on the days that I receive a letter from you. I can tell I have a letter from you before it gets into my hands because the mail clerk has a big smile when he comes up to me.*
>
> *The war news is wonderful. It should be over soon. It would be a great gift from God if it would end before Easter Sunday.*
>
> *…I am getting that spring feeling also and long more and more to be with you. Do you ever find me in your dreams? Most every night when I fall off to sleep I live over the times we were together – the things we did – what we said and the many things we should have said … Oh my sweet how I miss you. All my prayers are to get home in one piece to you…"*
>
> *All yours,*
> *Mitch*

Throughout the war, Mitch and A.J. sometimes sent each other gifts like the ring he sent from Rome, a jewel box from the island of Capri and gloves from Naples. After the war, A.J. told the kids about perhaps the most unique gift package Mitch received. She sent a bottle of liquor and this is how she did it: "You'd dig out the inside of the bread and put the bottle in and wrap it up good. You didn't want them to shake it and know what it was. In the bread, it would be fine."

Mitch loved it.

April 8, 1945

Dearest A.J.,

Today was a red letter day for me. I received two letters (wonderful letters) and a package from you. The package contained a wonderful bottle, which is at present being admired by two other officers. I don't know how long it will be before the top will come off. The two officers (Davis & Fish) are pleading with me to open it up. I think I have teased them enough so here goes. It is real good ... Just had another drink the second (both of them for you my sweet). Both Davis & Fish say thanks for your thoughtfulness."

Throughout the war, A.J.'s letters filled Mitch's heart, but the fighting was never far away.

... Oh! Anne I am praying for this war to end and to get home to you. The way it looks now Hitler is going to fight until the last German. I can't understand how a few men can have such control over a country when the majority

know that they are fighting for a lost cause. Such useless loss of life and limb. The Germans were supposed to be a smart race but … When they picked Hitler, that———— (fill in anything as long as it is real bad) is beyond me.

When you receive this letter we should be working real hard. Remember my sweet that I am always thinking of you and that you have all my love.

Yours,
Mitch

By April 1945, Mitch and the men of the Fifth Army were working "real hard." The final push of the war was underway. The combined might of the U.S. Fifth Army and British Eighth Army broke through the remaining German forces and poured into the Po Valley and up to the foothills of the Alps. Finally, on May 2nd, the war in Italy was officially over. Six days later May 8th, V-E Day—Victory in Europe – marked the end of hostilities throughout the continent. Mitch witnessed the victory and the final defeat of their implacable foe.

May 11, 1945

Dearest A.J.

Darling this is the first opportunity I had to write you since the wonderful defeat and surrender of the German Army. They were really beaten and out maneuvered.

I have so much to tell you that I don't know where to begin. I wish I could take off right now so I could tell it to you in person. My name was in to go home this month, but since the end of hostilities all temporary duty to the U.S. has been canceled ...

During this last drive we had many close calls and there were a few nights that I will never forget. The Bn. (battalion) was very lucky not one man was lost. The first few days were very rough, but then prisoners started to roll in by the thousands. Oh! It was wonderful to see. We all knew that the end was in store a week before it was announced. When it did come there was very little celebrating. Did the people at home do much in the way of celebrating? Our greatest thrill will be landing in the good old U.S.A. where our loved ones are.

At present we are located in Cortina d'Ampezzo in the Italian Alps. It is very beautiful. I don't think I have ever seen such scenery in all my travels. Oh! How I wish I could enjoy it with you. It may be soon now. The mountains all around are snow capped and the valley and low hills are green-green and just covered with flowers ...

My sweet I will close this letter as I have been interrupted so many times. Hoping to be one of the lucky ones and home soon to you.

All my love,
Mitch

At the end of the war, Mitch found himself to be the most senior officer in the Italian ski resort town of Cortina d'Ampezzo. Jet setters before and after the war made it their destination. Set in the Dolomite mountains, the scenery was spectacular. Mitch got along so well with the mayor, he wanted Mitch to stay or get married and come back. Mitch also learned the Germans had hidden a large stash of cognac and champagne. It's one war story the kids heard often. He succeeded in getting the senior German officer in town to tell him its location. Mitch shared it with his unit, and also found a way to ship some home for his soon coming wedding.

After the long Italian campaign, Mitch and the Fifth Army stood as victors, but at a great price. By the cease-fire of May 2nd, the Fifth Army had been engaged in continuous combat for more than 600 days, more than any other combat group during the war. They fought through rugged terrain, harsh, bitter weather, and a skilled and determined foe. It was a dogged advance of hundreds of miles. Throughout the war, nearly three quarters of a million men served in Italy. Total battle casualties reached more than 23,000 killed and nearly 100,000 wounded. Who knows how many Mitch's unit treated?

These were the men Tom Brokaw described in his best-selling book "The Greatest Generation." They shared a sense of kinship and did what they felt they were supposed to do. They fought for freedom. They fought to get home. They fought for their girls. "Mitch" fought for A.J.

For his service, Mitch was awarded the Bronze Star.
His citation reads:

SYLVESTER C. MITCHELL, First Lieutenant,
Medical Administrative Corps, United States Army.
For meritorious services in support of combat operations
from 10 September 1944 to 2 May 1945, in Italy.
Operating an ambulance control point, First Lieutenant

*Mitchell rendered praiseworthy service in the prompt
and efficient evacuation of wounded men. Displaying
keen foresight and resourcefulness, he made a sound and
equitable distribution of causalities among the hospitals,
insuring the most effective treatment of critical surgical
cases. The initiative and untiring devotion to duty of
First Lieutenant Mitchell are exemplary of the finest
traditions of the Medical Department of the United
States Army."*

In the Army's historical record of the 379th Medical Collecting Company, Mitch's unit received "battle honors for participation in the Sicily campaign during July 9, 1943 to August 17, 1943"; "battle credits for participation in the NAPLES-FOGGIA CAMPAIGN, 9 Sept.43 to 21 Jan 44, and the ROME-ARNO CAMPAIGN, 22 Jan 44 to … 10 Nov. 44; "battle participation for NORTH APENNINE CAMPAIGN from 19 Sept to 4 Apr 45 and for the PO VALLEY CAMPAIGN from 5 April 1945 to 8 May 45."[6] Note 6.

After the fighting, Mitch, like millions of other GI's, wanted to be home for Christmas. Their cry—"Home Alive in '45." In September, Mitch became part of the largest combined air and sealift ever organized, "Operation Magic Carpet." It officially commenced on September 6th, 1945, four days after V-J Day – Victory over Japan— and ended on September 1st, 1946. In a little less than a year, the U.S. Army arranged for eight million servicemen and women to return home from war theatres all over the globe. An average of "22,222

---

6   Department of the Army, U.S. Army Heritage and Education Center, Historical Data, 54th Medical Battalion, 379th Medical Collecting Company

"… The war news is wonderful. It should be over soon."

Americans home every day for nearly one year straight. The sum total provides the mathematical framework behind the beginning of the post-war Baby Boom nine months later."[7]

But who could go home, and when? To answer this question, the Army developed a point system where "every US soldier was awarded a number of points based on how long they had been overseas, how many decorations they had received, how many campaigns they had taken part in, and how many children they had."[8] For Mitch and others, "the points were all that mattered." 85 points punched you a ticket home. Anything under that meant you were likely headed to the U.S. for thirty days on furlough and then shipped to the Pacific to fight the unfinished – at the time—war with the Japanese.

On June 1st, Mitch wrote A.J. *"My possibilities of getting out of the Army look favorable at present. I have 107 points, which is fairly high among the officers of the Bn. (Battalion)"*

Then on July 15th, he sent her the good news. He would miss his "Band of Brothers," but he was headed home.

> *"The 379th is classified as a class II B unit which will go to the Pacific by way of the States. I was sorry to leave the Co. (Company) in a way but glad in another. Ever since I got my commission I was with this Company and have been very attached to it. But all the high point men have been transferred out which leaves only about 25% of the original company – men with under 85 points and I*

---

7   Note 8: "Home Alive By '45': Operation Magic Carpet, October 2, 2020, The National WWII Museum, New Orleans.

8   Note 7. Ibid.

*wouldn't like the idea of going to the States and spend 30
days on furlough and then get on a boat to the Pacific. I
feel that I have done my part and see no reason for going
to the Pacific. If for military reasons it was necessary then
I would feel different about it."*

Mitch continued.

*"We are now waiting for a boat. The way it looks now we
won't leave this area until the middle of August, but we
should be in the States the first part of Sept. Oh! happy
day ... Oh it is going to be so wonderful to get home
again and see you. I hope to get my discharge, but if I
don't I will have the first month home free. As soon as I
can get to a telephone I will call you. Don't have anything
planned for the whole month of Sept. I expect to end up at
Camp Devins from there I will call you. We will meet in
Boston – I will meet your family, then we will both take
off for Springfield – stay a few days and from there we can
make our plans together. Will close now my sweet one."
All my love, Mitch*

"The 379th departed Italy 24 Sep 45 On Joseph Nicolson (troop ship)
and arrived Hampton Roads Port of Embarkation per radio Leghorn
(Livorno), Italy."[9] Mitch had landed in Casablanca eight hundred
eighty-four days earlier on April 24th, 1943. His war was over, but the
romance went on and their plans came together quickly.

9   Ibid.

"… The war news is wonderful. It should be over soon."

A.J.'s Mom and Dad protested the wedding and said, "What are you rushing this poor boy to the altar so soon after the war?" But Mitch and A.J. would have none of it. On November 17th, 1945, Mitch and A.J. were married in St. Peter's Church in Dorchester, Massachusetts. Tom served as Mitch's Best Man and Elly as A.J.'s Maid of Honor. The champagne for the wedding came from Cortina. Like many other young couples after the war, they made do with living accommodations. They lived in various places including six months in the Hotel Edison in Lynn, Mass. But by the fall of the next year, they settled into their first new home, an apartment on 50 Humphrey Street on the border of Lynn and Swampscott, MA. It looked out over the Atlantic, the same ocean that kept them apart for three long years. But now they could walk its beaches and build the life they had longed for, hoped for, and prayed for. This new life deserved a good start and one last letter.

Nov. 20, 1946

My darling Wife,

I thought it would be proper and nice for me to be the sender of the first letter to you in our new home.

What memories are running thru my mind —Of the places where I used to be, and how far away you were when writing to you and how close you are now. This being my first letter to you since our marriage seems very strange esp. after leaving you this morning, in fact after just talking to you on the telephone about a chair for our home.

I wish so much for you and me. I hope that God will be good to us and protect and bless our home. I desire your happiness so much.

So my darling I wish you all the best in our new home.

Your loving,
Husband

God answered Mitch's prayer. He was good to them. He gave Mitch and A.J. four children and later seven grandchildren. They lived through the Cold War, survived the tumultuous '60s, endured financial setbacks, physical ailments and met the challenges of raising four children in an ever-changing world. Through 53 years of marriage, two constants remained: their unshakable faith in God and the enduring love they shared. It's been years since they've been here. But when their children re-discovered these letters—this long silent heritage come alive—they bore witness to the love that survived between Mitch and his "Dearest" A.J.

Dear Chris

"I was always so happy that you loved me."

Mitch and A.J. married for fifty three years

Dear Chris

"I was always so happy that you loved me."

Years after the war, Mitch took A.J. and his sister Peg to Italy and Sicily and showed them the places where he served. He took them to the beach at Gela, Sicily and the church where his driver was killed. They also visited the American cemetery at Anzio. "It was sad," A.J. would say, "hundreds and hundreds of crosses." These were the ones who didn't come home to their sweethearts.

Mitch was 27 when he entered the service and 32 when he got out. He gave some of the best years of his life, but he knew others who had given the "last full measure of devotion" would not be coming back. Mitch, like millions of other soldiers, faced the dangers and witnessed the horrors of war. This generation – called the "greatest" by some—rose to the challenge of their age and defeated the tyranny threatening the world. A.J. did say for the first couple of years of marriage, he would wake up in a sweat. But Mitch, like many veterans, seldom mentioned the war when he came back. There was a family to raise and a country to rebuild.

In Mitch's later years, he reflected on the great adventure of his life. He disliked war and what it did to men. Some wounds no medic could treat. Some went mad. His men risked their lives to drive the ambulances up and back from the front lines. He said some wounds looked fatal and men lived, while other wounds didn't look serious, yet men died. He lamented at what he felt was the incompetence of some of the generals above him and the waste of so many American lives. Decisions they made that cost many lives. He particularly criticized the Rapido River crossing on January 20-22, 1944. Considered an impossible suicide mission, troops had to cross a swift running river and scale heights to dislodge a dug-in enemy. It led to one of the greatest tragedies of the U.S. Army in the war. Of 4,000 troops, more than half were killed, captured, wounded or missing in action. The Germans lost only 64 men.

After the war, Mitch didn't return to Hills Brothers as a food chemist but co-owned a successful restaurant and bar in Lynn called "The Dubonnet." Some patrons called him "the priest" and he was so well liked, some wanted Mitch to run for mayor of Lynn. Later he ran a well-known Irish restaurant called "The Harp and Bard," on Boston's North Shore, where Mitch brought over many Irish entertainers.

Later in life, Mitch and A.J. spent ten years living in Las Vegas where Mitch still loved to play cards, this time not as "Captain Canteen" but as a patron at the Flamingo Casino poker room. But one year, both A.J. and Mitch got sick at the same time with no close family to care for them. That's when Kevin, Brian, Jeanne and Chris met and suggested to Mitch and A.J. to move east to Murphy, NC. They would be near Brian, a longtime physician at Murphy Medical Center. It was far from the action at the Flamingo, but Mitch still did manage to find a local poker game. They both loved being close to their two grandchildren, Kate and Anna, and driving distance from Chris, his wife Liz and son Philip.

October 31st, 1999 was Mitch's last day on earth. It was a full day which he spent watching Notre Dame beat Navy 28-24; played with his granddaughter Kate and enjoyed a spaghetti dinner. He visited A.J. in the hospital that day as well, since by this time she was frail and suffering from emphysema. Brian was with Mitch when he died.

When A.J. got the news, she was in shock, but she survived and the next summer visited his grave at the National Cemetery in Bourne, MA. At his funeral, Amazing Grace was played along with the Notre Dame fight song.

Mitch was gone but there was one more letter to be written and this time, it was A.J., who referred to Mitch also as Chris.

Dear Chris,

I used to wonder what life would be like without you. I know now how empty it can be. I think of you every day – all day and into the night. Life seems so meaningless. I look for you everywhere. I want to tell you everything but you're not there. I don't know how I can go on and live my life without you. I miss you so much. Weren't we lucky to have found one another and loved each other so much. I was always so happy that you loved me.

The tears are falling so often now when I know I must go on without you. I gained so much of my strength from you Chris. Whenever I had a problem you could always help me through it.

Our kids have been very supportive and close. I know that they all have their own grief to deal with and it's not easy when we are so far apart.

I was in denial after you died Chris. I just couldn't accept that you weren't here anymore. I talked about you as if you were still here. I know now that you are in heaven with God our Father and that you are looking down on us and helping us work through our grief. I think of all the times I should have, could have, been more aware of your physical limitations. Oh, what a lonely life without you.

Folks at church are so sweet. They are so kind. I know that they feel my pain so it is a warm environment to be in.

A.J. never finished her letter. Perhaps the tears began to flow again.

Kevin retired to Fort Myers, FL, after a long career in the restaurant business, gaming industry and real estate. Brian still serves the medical needs of the people of Cherokee County, NC, at Peachtree Medical Clinic, where he has practiced for more than forty years. Jeanne retired after many years as a special needs teacher in Lynn, MA. Chris still serves as the Bureau Chief for CBN News in Jerusalem.

They all miss Mitch and A.J.

Mitch's Letters

April 19, 1943

APRIL 19, 1943

Dear Ann,

Please excuse the delay in answering your most welcome letter.

Before I left my last station I said goodbye to Fr. Heamer.

I haven't seen Finnen for the last five days and I really miss him.

There is so much to say hut it is impossible to say it due to censorship. It is terrible writing a letter with such a restriction over one's head.

The weather has been very warm the last few days; in fact I am getting a sunburn.

81

DEAREST A.J.

*I would love to he in New York this coming weekend—
dancing at the Plaza etc.*

*The card games have been fast and furious and I am still
managing to hold my own.*

I received the check you sent—it really wasn't necessary.

*Excuse the writing—I have a bad hand but not this bad.
Let's blame it on the working.*

Well Ann I will close hoping all is well.

*Love,
Mitch*

MAY 8, 1943

Dear Ann,

Arrived safely somewhere in North Africa. When this messed up world settles down I will be able to tell you in the fullest detail the episodes of my travels.

Our trip over was very quiet and uneventful Although one of the other companies had quite a lot of excitement.

Did you receive my last letter? It was written in Bermuda, where we had a few days stop. I meant to send you some perfume from there but we left the day I intended to get it.

The Red Cross is doing a wonderful job in this war. Do not fail to give to them.

From what I have seen of these North African Cities or in/act any of the places where I have been I am left with the feeling of appreciation that I come from the good old U.S.A.

The country around here is beautiful but the people are filthy. The Arabs run around with rags wrapped around them. The population is comprised of Arabs, French, and Moslems.

I am writing this letter from our new camp, which is located on the side of a hill overlooking a large vineyard grove.

We just received the good news that the African campaign has come to a successful conclusion.

I was in town this afternoon where I enjoyed a few beers in a beer garden located on the sidewalk. While in town I ran into some friends from my old outfit.

This morning I changed all my American money into this exchange. Now I have so much paper money that I could wallpaper two large rooms. All we can buy with it is wine and beer and a few other unessentials.

May 8, 1943

How about seeing you in New York this coming weekend? I could really go for a good steak. But I would much rather see you.

Well AJ I will close hoping I receive a letter from you soon.

Love,
Mitch

JUNE 8, 1943

Dear Anne,

*Enclosed you will find a few postcards of the ruins of
Agrigento, Sicily. These are 532B.C. old. This city was
captured by the Greeks, Romans, Carthagenians many
times and now by the Americans.*

*The news of Italy's surrender just came over the radio.
Gee it really makes us all feel so good. We have felt this
was going to happen as we had seen some Italian planes
land at one of the Sicilian airports. We had a report a
few weeks ago of an Italian cruiser, which was allowed to
sail fairly close to the Sicilian coast, unhampered when it
could have been easily disposed of.*

*Yesterday I received three letters from you, which I will
answer tomorrow.*

Love,
Mitch

Aug. 19, 1943

Dear Ann Jean;

Please excuse the very long delay in writing to you. This delay is in no way an indication of lapse of memory, for you have been on my mind from one night in Boston. Since I put foot on this Island I have been so busy, only getting a few hours sleep in 24 hours, that letter writing was really impossible.

I landed on, D-Day, which means the 1st day, July 1(lh about ten miles east of Gela. Tomorrow I will write you a long letter about my trip from North Africa.

In my travels thru this mountainous Island I bought you a present which I will mail when I get back to the Co. I have been away from the Co. for the last few days.

So much has happened and it is still forbidden to tell all that it makes letter writing very difficult.

87

Ann I will close this short note as I am very tired for I have traveled 125 miles over these rough mountainous roads today.

Wishing I were near you.

Love,
Mitch

OCT. 22, 1943

Dear Anne,

Just received your letter of Sept 16, which increased my morale greatly.

Please excuse the writing as I am still in a horizontal position in bed. I was out of the hospital for five days but was forced to return when my malaria reoccurred. I am feeling fine now and am sure this present treatment will rid me of this — malaria.

I would love to be with you and prove to you that you aren't suffering from any delusions. If my letters have failed to convey that I do miss you and are constantly thinking of you I am sorry. Most of my letters are always cut and dry.

You will notice that my APO# has been changed to 464.

xxxxxxxxxxxxxxxxxxxxxxxxxxxxxxxxxxxxxxxxxxxxxxx

While in the hospital I received your package of Yardley's soap, which is quite a rarity over here. Thanks for the package. Send some snapshots of yourself in your next letter. I would love to see the movie roll we took in New York, my sister said it was good.

Today the weather is perfect for a football game.

Someday we will be able to see some good game together. Will close honey for now.

With all my love,
Mitch

NOV. 10, 1943

Dear A.J.

Somewhere in Sicily

*Still in the hospital but expect to be out within a week or
so. I am starting to get my appetite back, but wish I were
back in the States where I could get some good food.*

*Last night I heard a rebroadcast of the Hit Parade, in
which they played our song, "You Would be so Nice to
Come Home to"—it really made me homesick.*

*It is getting fairly cool over here now and being in tents
doesn't help much. This is a tent hospital, but is relatively
comfortable, due to the fact that we have spring beds and
a nice mattress to go with it and oh yes linen also—these
were all captured from the Italians.*

*By the time I catch up with my outfit I should have quite
a bit of mail waiting for me. I hope you have sent those
pictures I asked for.*

Have you seen any good football games? I would love to have seen the Army and Notre Dame game with you. This is the first year I missed that game in about five years.

Well honey I will close.

With all my love,
Mitch

NOV. 12. 1943

Dear A.J.

Still somewhere in Sicily

I am still in the hospital but I hope to be out within a few days.

This morning I sent for some Xmas cards in a town close by, which I just finished addressing. I sent you the best one I could find.

I am anxious to catch up with my outfit, my promotion should have been back by now, and I should have a lot of mail waiting for me.

My day in the hospital consists of reading and playing cards. My luck at cards has been exceptionally good except for yesterday which was very unsuccessful.

In the Stars and Stripes an Army newspaper, I read the results of the Army-Notre Dame football game. I would

93

have loved to have been there (avec vous). Notre Dame must have a bang-up team.

Thanksgiving will be only a few days away by the time you receive this letter. Have a piece of turkey for me.

A.J. I really miss you and anxiously waiting for the day when we can be together again.

I will close this short note hoping you well.

With all my love,
Mitch

NOV. 17, 1943

Dear Ann Jean,

Still in the hospital and have given up guessing as to when I will get out. This morning I asked the doctor when I will get out, his answer wasn't to encouraging "a week or two." I am sure I will be out before that as I am getting sick of this place.

My promotion came thru this morning it was sent back to me from the outfit. It was dated Sept. 17—so I have been a 1ˢᵗ Lt. from that date.

I am anxious to get back to the outfit to get some of my mail. I hope your pictures are there or did you send them yet?

It gets very monotonous lying here all day with nothing to do. In /act even with the outfit becomes very tiring after staying in one place for a week or more. Since I have been here I have been doing a lot of thinking and daydreaming—mostly of you. I would love to get home even for a 2-month vacation—that's pipe dreaming.

Well darling I will close this short note hoping you are well.

All my love,
Mitch

NOV. 21, 1943

Dearest A.J.

Somewhere in Italy

Just caught up with my outfit yesterday. I found seven of your letters waiting for me and your package. Your letters were dated from Sept. 7ᵗʰ to Nov. 8ᵗʰ. Thanks a lot honey. I will try to answer one of your letters each day—so here goes for your Sept 7 letter—first I will take time out to read it again (fifth time). By the way I am feeling O.K.

I liked the paragraph in which you said how much you missed me. That is the way I want you to feel, but I hope we both don't have to feel that way too long, this mess will end soon. Let's hope and pray it will.

You mentioned the night we were at the Plaza together. What I wouldn't give to be back there with you right now.

It was snowing that night but it was a good snow.

Honey send a few snap shots of yourself, if you don't have any have some taken. Have them about the size that would fit inside a cigarette case—that could be carried with me.

I flew over from Sicily—someday soon I hope I will be able to tell you about the trip.

I feel bad about not being able to send you something nice for Xmas. I should find something nice in Italy to send you.

Will close honey until tomorrow.

All yours,

Love
Mitch

NOV. 22, 1943

Dearest A.J.

Somewhere in Italy

Just reread your letter of Sept 13. I will answer so many of the questions you asked as possible. Some I can't answer because of censorship. Also honey there is so much I would love to write about but regulations say no.

I saw Finnen recently and he is fine, just as jovial as ever. When we are operating I don't see him very often because we don't operate together.

As you know by the news the weather is terrible. I never saw so much mud.

You asked about receiving mail from home—on the average I received about two to three letters from Peg, Pat, or mother a week. Much more than I write—as you know—but I am improving.

DEAREST A.J.

In one of my latest letters from home they spoke about the movie films we took in New York, Central Park etc.— remember? Peg said that my mother liked you very much from the film—she also said that the film came out very good. Of course I knew mother couldn't help but like the sweetest little thing on earth.

In your letter of Sept 13 you mentioned about Gallagher's steaks not being as large. Honey right now just one mouth full would be appreciated.

Hurry up and send a snapshot not one—two. Will close until tomorrow.
All my love,
Mitch

NOV 23, 1943

My Dear A.J.

Somewhere in Italy

This is in answer to your letter of Sept. 23. Really honey it was a wonderful letter. You sure poured your heart out and I love it. I find it hard to put on paper what I feel for you. I hope you can read between the lines and that soon I will be able to explain or show my love in other ways than on paper.

I am feeling fine and am beginning to put on a little weight. In my letters home I made the mistake of telling mother that I was in the hospital with malaria and I had the mildest form of the mildest type. But I imagine the word malaria is enough to frighten anyone, but those who have my medical training. Atraleine is now used as a care instead of quinine.

DEAREST A.J.

This afternoon I received a fruitcake from home. We had it for supper and it was very good.

The handkerchiefs you sent were very nice and came in handy. I also needed the ties but don't know when I will be able to wear them.

Well honey I am going to get a little shut eye. I will dream of you till I fall asleep.

All my love,
Mitch

NOV. 25, 1943

Dearest A.J.

Sorry to miss writing yesterday but it was an impossibility.

Went to Mass this morning. It was a nice service with music and singing. After mass we had Benediction. Our chaplain is a swell egg, a Polish fellow, Fr. Waraska. He plays a good game of poker and he loves his liquor.

Saw Finnen at Mass and hope to see him this afternoon He is fine. Lt Taylor is troubled with his right hand and left leg. You remember the night I called him on the phone at the Hotel Statler.

To our surprise our Thanksgiving turkeys came in last night. We are having them for dinner. What I wouldn't give to be having my Thanksgiving with you. I will think of you during the whole meal.

DEAREST A.J.

In your letter of Oct 11 you mentioned your dad being ill. I hope it isn't serious and that he is feeling well now.

I am waiting for those two snapshots. I would like to be carrying your picture around with me. When my morale gets low I could look at your picture and it would pick me right up.

Last night before falling to sleep I kept thinking about the day we will meet again in the States—where it will be Boston—New York. What we will do etc.

Will close honey until tomorrow.

I miss you so much

Love,
Mitch

Nov. 26, 1943

NOV. 26, 1943

Dearest A.J.

Somewhere in Italy

Your letter of Oct. 18 was very thrilling about your trip to Springfield. But I was disappointed that you didn't call up Peg or Pat and meet my mother. She would have loved to meet you. You would have been able to see the film we took in New York. The next time you are in Springfield make sure you give Peg or Pat a ring. In my letter home I didn't say you were in Springfield (because Peg would be hurt). That train from Springfield and Boston is all you say and more. There is one train worse than that one you took—it takes almost four hours stopping every 100 feet or so.

Finnen took a few snapshots of me but I don't know if he has them developed. If he does I will send you them. I am still waiting for yours. Come on honey send me an image of your beautiful face with that little turned up nose.

I had three letters yesterday from my sister Rita. She is in Little Rock, Arkansas with her husband who is an officer in the Inf. You will meet her someday. She is ok I am sure you will like her.

Well Honey will close until tomorrow. Hoping all is well with you and that your Dad is better.

All my love,
Mitch

Nov. 29, 1943

NOV. 29, 1943

Dearest A.J.

Just returned from my first trip to a nearby town and found your letter of the 12ᵗʰ waiting for me. What are you trying to do to me run me competition being laid up in bed? Really Anne I hope it isn't serious. You didn't say much about it. Just that you had an accident and are under a doctor's care. Were you driving fast? Peg is a good driver but she drives too fast. Everytime I ride with her my heart is in my mouth, but I would never tell her.

A few nights ago I said my prayers. Someday I will tell you about it. While in town I bought you a few presents, which I will mail to you tomorrow. I hope you will like them. I will tell you what they are, because you will receive this letter about 3 weeks before the presents. First there are two pairs of gloves. One is a pair of black and white—

107

DEAREST A.J.

Oh I don't know what kind of material; the other is a long white kid evening gloves. I am sure you will like the latter. I was going to buy you some perfume but I don't know good perfume from bad and I was afraid of getting stuck. A link bracelet with four cameos, and two unmounted cameos... one for a ring and the other on a chain. The mounting here is terrible as all the gold has disappeared.

Darling please excuse the writing as I am writing in close quarters.

As present I am feeling fine and beginning to get back some of my lost weight.

In your last letter you mentioned sending your portrait. I haven't received it I will be waiting for it in every mail call.

Hope you are OK from your misfortunate accident. Drive careful, watch out crossing the street, and stay away from 4F's until I come home.

Love,
Mitch

DEC. 2, 1943

Dear Anne,

Somewhere in Italy

Please excuse these v-mail letters I have been writing, when I get time I will write a real letter.

We haven't received any mail for the last few days so when the mailman arrives I hope I have a few letters from you.

I believe that in my last letter I told you that Lt Taylor is no longer with us. He has gone back to the States.

The day before yesterday I mailed your package, I hope you like the contents.

I am writing this letter in a tent, which is situated in an orange grove. It is possible to reach out and pick a nice ripe orange.. I have already eaten my share. It is now 7 o'clock and off in the distance the artillery can be heard.

They are really laying it on. You get so accustomed to the noise that when it stops you feel a little uneasy.

It hard to realize the month of Dec. is here already, especially when there is no snow on the ground.

From what I have seen of this country of course it hasn't been much, but still, I can't for the life of me see why that fatheaded Mussolini ever stuck his chest out or opened his big mouth. Today I saw a little girl barefooted, no more than 12 years old, plowing a field with two oxen—nice work if you can get it. The women over here do more work than the men or as much. Of course in the States at present we have women doing everything but mining.

Well my sweet one I will close until tomorrow.

All yours,
Mitch

DEC. 24, 1943

Dearest A.J.

I received your letter containing the snapshots. One of which I cut down to fit my cigarette case, so everytime I have a cigarette I must first take a look at you. As of yet I haven't received the large picture; it may be in the mail tonight (the mail clerk just left—I told him not to come back without a letter from you).

I just finished censoring some of the Company mail and by their letters the men are a little homesick. It is tough to spend Xmas here with artillery in lieu of sleigh bells, but it could be much worse. First we should be thankful to be alive and well, and we are much better off then most of the Italian people whose homes and towns are left in a pile of debris by war.

Honey I am a little homesick and hope and pray that next Xmas I will be home and with you.

111

Did you receive the package I sent you? I hope you like the gloves.

Well Honey I will close this short note and will write tomorrow.

All my love,
Mitch

DEC. 25, 1943

Dearest A.J.

I have been thinking about you most of the day.

What you are doing etc. I hope your Xmas was a pleasant and happy one.

Today we had a wonderful Xmas dinner. It is unbelievable what can be done in the field a few miles behind the lines. We sat down to a table with a clean white linen tablecloth. The menu consisted of roast turkey, which was delicious, mashed potatoes, mashed sweet potatoes, peas and carrots, dressing, giblet gravy, white and raisin bread, fresh butter, fresh fruit, oranges, apples, and almond nuts, wonderful cherry and raisin pies, cookies formed in stars, Xmas trees and crosses, coffee and wine. What do you think of that for a menu? Oh yes we had the echo of artillery for music.

On a clear day, which is seldom, the scenery is beautiful. High white capped mountain ranges and deep green fertile valleys.

But the weather spoils all its beauty, rain day after day.

Everyone in the company except the guards have gone to bed so I will join the rest and jump into my sleeping bag and dream of Boston or 10 Bullard St.

Goodnight my sweet one,

Love,
Mitch

Dear A.J.

Please excuse the delay in writing but circumstances are such that writing is difficult. I am feeling fine and there is no need of worrying.

You haven't as yet mentioned receiving any of my packages.

The weather has improved the last few days. I hope it stays that way.

In your last letter you mentioned the episodes of your little sister. She must be some girl. Don't let her know I called her little sister, she may not like it.

I hope and pray that this mess will be over soon. I have seen all I want to see. The U.S. will really look good to me, so will you. Won't we do the rounds the day I get my feet on that precious soil? You know dear the people in the U.S. don't know how lucky they are.

Honey I hope my letters don't sound or read depressing.

Hope all is well.

I love you

Love,
Mitch

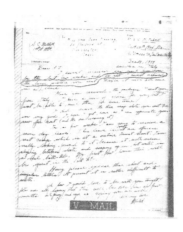

JAN. 14, 1944

Dear A.J.

Somewhere in Italy

I haven't received any mail from you for the last few weeks and as yet I haven't received the large picture you sent. Maybe it will all come in a bunch.

Have you received the package I sent you from Italy? I have a pair of gloves for you, but I won't be able to mail them for some time.

I did receive the three snap shots you sent. One was very good. I hope I get home so I can appreciate your new fur coat (and the one wearing it).

In a few weeks I am going to receive a seven-day leave. This leave is spent at an officer's rest camp, which is at a onetime tourist resort. I am really looking forward to it because it will mean sleeping between sheets and soaping up in hot water in a real bath-tub. My first few hours there will be spent in the bath-tub.

Honey please excuse these short and irregular letters. At present it is rather difficult to write.

Oh how I would love to be with you tonight. We are all hoping that this will be over in a few months. Let's pray and hope so. Hoping you are well.

All my love,
Mitch

Dearest A.J.

Just a short note before I hit the hay. I am very sleepy, as I didn't get much shut-eye last night.

I haven't received a letter from you for quite sometime — pourquoi (French for why)? Honey maybe I haven't any right to complain as I should write you more often, but I do look forward to receiving your letters.

The weather has been wonderful for the last few days or maybe it is just the marked difference that makes me think it is wonderful. As you may know by the paper, we did have some terrible weather.

This war should be over this year with God's help. When that day comes I will be thinking of you and of a fast way back to the States. New York will look good with you on my arm.

119

Will close now my beautiful one and get into my sleeping bag — hoping to dream of you.

All my love,
Mitch

Darling A.J.

Received your two letters of Jan. 25 today, which lifted my morale, no end Honey here is a poem, which I thought, was worth sending you — hope you like it.

I
Sitting on my G.I. bed
My G.I. hat upon my head,
My G.I. pants, my G.I. shoes
Everything free nothing to lose
G.I. razor, G.I. comb,
G.I. wish that I were home.

II
They issue everything we need,
Paper to write on, books to read
They issue food to make you grow,
G.I. want a long furlough.

III
Your belt, your shoes, your G.I. tie
Everything free nothing to buy
You eat your food from G.I. plates
Buy your needs, at G.I. rates.

IV
It's G.I. this and G.I. that
G.I. haircut, G.I. hat
Everything here is Government Issue
G.I. wish that I could kiss you.

Will Write tomorrow

All my love,
Mitch

FEB. 18, 1944

Dearest A.J.

Somewhere in Italy

*Please excuse the long delay in writing but really honey it
was impossible to write the last week or so. Right now we
are having a breather, in fact we just finished playing a
game of volleyball.*

*I received your letter of February 4 in which you told of
your visit to Springfield. Oh darling how I wish I were
with you. My sister Pat who likes you very much wrote me
about your visit.*

*A few days ago I sent you a jewel box and a pair of white
gloves. I hope you like them.*

*I had a very good time at the Officers Rest Center, but
it was impossible to rest when you knew you were on
borrowed time and that in a few days you would be back*

*"sweating them out" (waiting along for shells to come in).
I stayed in a beautiful hotel with a room overlooking the
sea. The meals were wonderful, with music added The
drinks were only fair. What a wonderful set up if you were
with me and this _____ war was over with.*

*Pat said you were wearing the pendant I sent you from
Sicily. She said it looked nice on the black dress you were
wearing.*

Well A.J. will close for now hoping that your dad is better.

*All my love,
Mitch*

Feb. 19, 1944

FEB. 19, 1944

Dearest A.J.

Right at present I am very lonely and would give a lot to have you in my arms to tease and make love to. But we will have to suffer and wait until these _____ _____ Germans quit. I hope it won't be to long.

At present we have a fairly good setup with very little to do. Today was passed playing volleyball and checkers. We have daily Mass in our present area. Finnen is nearby and the poker games are going to commence again. I would be able to give you more details on our present set up but censorship won't allow.

The weather has changed for the better but it is still cool From where I am writing this letter I can look in any direction and see snow capped mountains.

Yesterday I went to a nearby town I should day city and had a bath in a real bathtub. It was wonderful. I used a whole bar of the soap you sent me. I wasn't that dirty, but it was so good that I stayed in the tub for about an hour.

Well Darling will close until tomorrow.

All my love,
Mitch

FEB. 22, 1944

Dearest A.J.

I have been sitting by a fire for the last fifteen minutes reading some of your letters, which I have been saving. Just finished reading the letter where you mentioned receiving the cameos. I am glad you liked them. I am sure they will look nice on you—you cute thing. I think of you constantly and long for the day of our reunion. Many times have I thought how nice it would be to be able to go to the phone and say honey, "how about meeting me in New York?" Or to be dancing with you at the Plaza.

In your letter you mentioned how hard you are working — now take it easy. You don't want me to come home and find you worn down from work. The women over here do more work than the men. The other day a woman and her husband walked by our area. The woman was carrying a big log of wood on her head and the man was walking behind her with nothing in his hands, and that is a common occurrence.

The mail just came in and I received your Valentine.

Honey I was unable to send one, but you are my Valentine—with all my heart.

From one who cares.

All my love,
Mitch

March 29, 1944

MARCH 29, 1944

Dear Anne

Will write tomorrow

I love you

Italy 1944 Happy Easter

Love,
Mitch

APRIL 6, 1944

Dearest A.J.

Today is one of those beautiful days, which comes in Spring. It is warm and everything seems so alive that my thoughts were only for you. Thus this letter instead of a small v-mail

You may have noticed the change in address. We changed a little in organization but are operating the same as before. We are now a separate company, which means that we can operate independently of headquarters.

Everyone that sees your picture likes it very much. In fact Weiner is looking at it right now. You remember him—he was with us when we went to "Cafe Society" in the Village.

The mail just came in. Here's hoping I receive a letter from you.

From my last letter from home I learned that my brother is

April 6, 1944

on his way over here. I feel sorry for him, as it is tough for Inf. Replacements. They get tossed around from replacement pool to replacement pool and are so green when they do hit a permanent outfit, which is usually on the line.

Just received you letter of March 12ᵗʰ in which you said my letters are the brightest spot of your life. Honey I hope that spot grows.

Everytime I look at your picture I long to get home to you.

In your letter you mentioned seeing pictures of the bombing of the monastery atop Mt Cassino. I would like to see those pictures as I had a birds eye view of the same. That should answer your question.

Is Elly still in New York? New York is alright to visit but not to live in. It can be very lonely esp. for a girl

I received an Easter Card from your Mother and Dad. It was nice.

Thank them for me, and I thank you for your card I will be thinking of you this Easter. Let us hope and pray that next Easter we will be together.

I do miss you very much, and long for the day of my return when I can be with you. Honey that will be a happy day for me.

Write soon —all my love.
Mitch

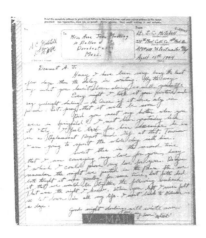

APRIL 15, 1944
Dearest A.J.

Honey I have been very busy the last few days thus the delay in writing. By the way my sweet you haven't been doing so well yourself.

Every night I look at your picture and say goodnight darling—oh Anne if it were only in person. Lets pray that it will be soon.

Did you meet my brother when you were in Springfield? I met him yesterday here in Italy. I feel for him because he is in a replacement depot and infantry at that. Tomorrow I am going to spend the whole day with him.

Sweet this is the second time that I am conveying my love for you, honey I wish I could prove my love for you. Do you remember the night we parted in the Penn. Sta.

We both thought it was goodby for some time, but fate had it that we would be together the following weekend. That was the night I knew. When you left I never felt so let down in all my life. I went back to Kolner in a daze.

Good night darling—will write soon.

All my love,
Mitch

APRIL 22, 1944

Dearest A.J.

Honey it has been quite sometime since I received a letter—
maybe I am complaining—but I do appreciate your letters
so. They remind me that you are thinking and waiting for
me. As far as letter writing goes I am one that shouldn't
complain because I write so little. In f act I started to write
this letter two days ago, but just couldn't get to it Honey
don't judge my love to the amount of letters I write you. If
you did I would have to be writing all the time.

Yesterday I saw my brother for the second time. He is fine,
but right now is in a Replacement Pool, which is like
being a little stone on a beach waiting for someone to pick
you up. I am trying to get someone to pick you up. I am
trying to get him into the Bn. I hope I am successful.

DEAREST A.J.

Have you heard from Pat? Or have you visited Springfield recently? It has been a week since I received a letter from home. Maybe the mailman stopped in for a beer. Usually I receive two letters a week from home.

April 24, 1944

APRIL 24, 1944

A few days has elapsed since I started this letter– reason— the night I started the generator went dead and yesterday was a very busy day.

Since I started this letter my brother has been assigned to the Bn. Isn't that a break? I thank God that I was in a position to help him out Later I hope to get him into the Finance Dept. where he can put his training to good use both for himself and the Army.

Last week a number of enlisted men in our Bn. Received awards for heroic achievements in combat We have one man who is in for the "Legion of Merit" we hope he will receive it soon.

I received a letter from home today dated the 13th of April and they didn't mention receiving flowers I sent for Easter. I am sure they would have mentioned it if they

137

had received them. I hope you received my flowers. I had visions of you wearing them Easter Sunday. Honey let me know if and when you received them.

Well my sweet one I will close with a promise to write a V mail tomorrow. I hope that this mess is over soon so I can get home to you.

All my love,
Mitch

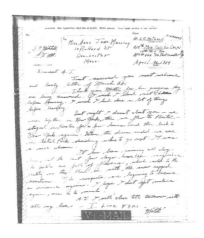

APRIL 26, 1944

Dearest A.J.

Just received your most welcome and lovely letter of March 28.

Thank your mother for her prayers—they are being answered. I wish I had met her before leaving. I wish I had done a lot of things before leaving.

Last night I dreamt about you we were together in New York, then we flew to Boston, stayed in Boston for a few hours and then back to New York again. When the dream ended we were in Central Park deciding where to go next. It was a nice dream.

It has been raining all day here, but the last few days have been very nice. The fields are full of flowers, which add to the beauty as they blend in with the snow capped mountains. The mosquitoes are beginning to become a nuisance again. I hope I don't get malaria again, once is too much.

A.J. I will close till tomorrow with all my love.

I love Vous,
Mitch

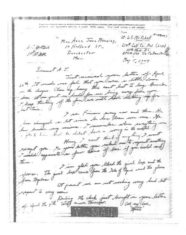

MAY 5, 1944

Dearest A.J.

Just received your letter of April 20th. It made me feel that you were a little down in the dumps. Cheer up honey this can't last to long. Remember dear it is just as hard for me being away from you. I keep thinking of the fun we will have making up for lost time.

I see Finnen every now and then. He has changed a lot since he has been over seas. He has become very serious. I remember when everything was a joke to him and he didn't have a worry in the world.

Honey I can't think of anything I want except you. In your letter you asked me to request something. I would appreciate a few cans of beer if you could send them.

I am glad you liked the jewel box and the gloves. The jewel box came from the Isle of Capri and the gloves from Naples.

At present we are not working very hard but expect to very soon.

Darling the clerk just brought in your letter of April the 9th. Will answer tomorrow.

All my love,
Mitch

May 7, 1944

Dearest A.J.

*Honey today I received your letter of April 9th. It is
strange how I received it so late, when I received your
letter of the 23rd a few days ago. I was disappointed that
you didn't receive my flowers for Easter Sunday.*

*Tonight there is a beautiful full moon. I am sitting here
looking at it and I can think of a lot more places where I
would love to look at this same moon. All of them would
be with you.*

*I am glad you didn't join the service, and date. Of course
I would love to have you over here, but it would be purely
selfish on my part as I might be able to see you once a
month. Maybe I am not being patriotic but darling one of
us is enough to be away from the things we love, the things
we are used to, and the things our young boys are dying
for. The Wacs don't have it bad over here. They live in nice
quarters, I imagine they eat well, but it still isn't anything*

like home. I am sure they would rather be back home.

*Darling it isn't true that after eighteen months overseas
duty you will be sent home. There is a rotation plan in
affect which allows ½ of 1 % of the command to be
rotated a month. Of this 90% for unlisted personnel and
10% for officers. As yet no officers from our Bn hos been
rotated but we have sent some EM home.*

Will write tomorrow.

All my love,
Mitch

MAY 19, 1944

Dearest A.J.

Darling please excuse the delay in writing we have been very busy for the last week or so, thus I have been unable to even write a short V-mail.

All my thoughts are of you, every night when I fall off to sleep you are on my mind. I recall the times we were together, the things we did. How fate was so unkind to separate us so soon. If we only had a few more months together. I don't know how many times during the day I wish I was with you. Darling I am serious—I was never so serious. I never was in love until one night in Boston. I was very sure I loved you when tears came to my eyes when I left you at the Grand Central Station. Do you remember? We had a hard time getting a berth. I would give a lot to be with you now.

In one of Pat's recent letters she said she hoped to see you soon. When she and Peg were in New York they missed seeing Elly.

Darling it shouldn't be too long before we are together again. Let's both pray that the time will be short and pass fast.

I am in good health—no pain except a big spot in my heart.

All my love,
Mitch

June 9, 1944

Dearest A.J.

Somewhere in Italy

I should start this V mail by bawling you out for not writing. Darling it has been quite sometime since I heard from you and I do look forward to reading your letters. Words can't describe my desire to get home to you and how I miss you.

From the papers and radio and my lack of writing you know we are very busy. Both Tom and I are fine. At present we are having a little rest after a very strenuous month.

What did you think of the Invasion News? We were thrilled here especially when it came at the same time as the fall of Rome. I hope and pray that it is successful and that this mess will be over soon with very little bloodshed

147

DEAREST A.J.

This morning I sent you a ring as a souvenir of a great city. I hope you like it. All my love goes with it.

I could write so much but censorship wouldn't approve.

Did you receive the orchid I sent you for Easter yet? I was very disappointed that you didn't receive them for Easter.

Well darling will close with all my love. Hoping you are well.

Write often

Love,
Mitch

Dearest A.J.

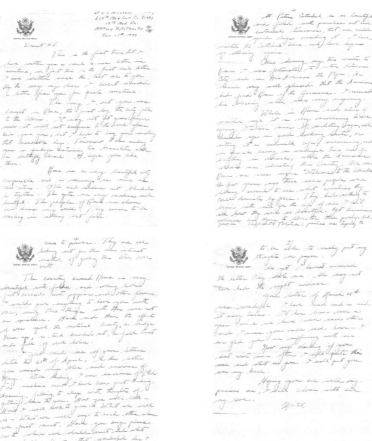

This is the first time that I have written you a real he-
man letter in sometime; inf act this is the first real letter I
have written since the last one to you. By the way my dear
I haven't received a letter from you for quite sometime.

The ring I sent you was bought in Rome, the first day the city fell to the Allies. It may not fit your finger and it will not compare to the rock your Dad gave you, but I had to buy you something that memorable day. Tomorrow I am sending you a package containing two bracelets and a butterfly broach. I hope you like them.

Rome is a very beautiful city comparable and in someways as nice as our cities. Old and modern art blended in together. The apts. are very modern and beautiful The people of Rome are clean and dress very well They seem to be wanting in nothing but food. St Peter's Cathedral is so beautiful and filled with priceless art and historical treasures, that one could spend days visiting it. I have visited the Cathedral twice and have hopes of returning again.

Also during my two visits to Rome I was fortunate to enter Vatican City and see His Holiness the Pope. He seemed very well pleased that the Americans had freed Rome of the Germans. I received his blessing, which was very inspiring.

While in Rome and cities of similar size it is very maddening to see young Italian men of military age, all dressed up in good looking suits, or sitting at a sidewalk cafe, swimming, and in general having a wonderful time as if everything is normal, while American soldiers are liberating their country. All over Rome one sees signs "Welcome to the Liberators." A few years ago these same people were looking around to see what countries they could dominate by force. They had nothing to begin with and for the life of me I cant see how they were so boastful Yet American soldiers are dying to liberate these poorly led people. Different political parties are trying to come to power. They are all looking out for there own interest instead of getting this war over with.

DEAREST A.J.

The country around Rome is very beautiful with fields and rolling hills just covered with poppies and other flowers. I would give anything to have you with me, seeing these things with this war not in existence. Here and there the effects of war spoil the natural beauty, a bridge blown up, a tank knocked out, a field burnt and full of shell holes.

I just read one of your letters dated the 20th of April In this letter you seemed very blue and envious of Mary. Well darling I am envious of Phil For sometime now I have been just thinking, dreaming, falling to sleep with thoughts of getting home to you. How you will look—How I will look to you—What we will do—What we will say to each other when we first meet. Have you any plans as to where we should meet and what we should do on that wonderful day? I think of you so much, but I never seem to be able to really put my thoughts on paper.

June 15, 1944

As yet I haven't received the letter Elly wrote me. She may not have had the right address.

Your letter of March 28th was wonderful I have read and re-read it many times. It has been over a year since we have seen each other and I miss you more each hour—I am glad you are suffering with me.

Now darling if you don't write more often I will quit this war and start on you. I will put you over my knee.

Hoping you are well my precious one, I will close with all my love.

Mitch

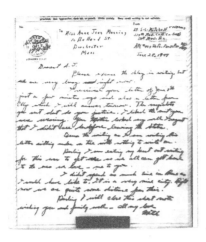

JUNE 28, 1944

Dearest A.J.

Please excuse the delay in writing, but we are very busy right now.

I received your letter of June 9ᵗʰ just a few minutes ago and also a letter from Elly, which I will answer tomorrow. The snapshots you sent don't do you justice. I liked the suit you were wearing. Your mother looked very well I regret that I didn't see her before leaving the States.

Excuse the writing as I am writing this letter sitting under a tree with nothing to write on.

Darling I am eating my heart out waiting for this war to get over so we all can get home to the ones we love me to you.

I didn't spend as much time in Rome as I would have like to. It is a very nice city. Right now we are quite some distance from there.

Darling I will close this short note wishing you and family well—

All my love,
Mitch

JULY 19, 1944

Dearest A.J.

*Darling please excuse the long delay between my short
letters, when I get home I will be able to explain the
reason. You are in my mind continually; you are my ray of
light in this dark world.*

*We all feel that it will be over soon now, by the end of this
year anyway. At present here in Italy the Germans are fighting
back very hard. They know that they have lost the war and for
the life of me I can't see why they continue fighting.*

*I continually visualize the day I will get back home to
you. Oh darling it will be wonderful. I am going to need
a long rest and plenty of good food and of course you first.
I never dreamt it would be for so long.*

July 19, 1944

We haven't received any mail for the last two weeks so I am going to look for a pile of letters all-together.

Will try to write tomorrow.

All my love,
Mitch

JULY 19, 1944

Dear Elly,

Please excuse the delay in answering your most welcome letter. At present it is very difficult to find time or to be in the proper mood to write a half way decent letter. In your letter (you) mentioned that it doesn't seem possible that I have been overseas so long. Really Elly it is a long time to be away from the ones you love. I knock myself out every night thinking of Anne and the time I will get home to her. At present the war news is_ good and the end seems to be in sight.

July 19, 1944

How do you like living in the big city? I always liked to visit New York, but I wouldn't like to make my home there. Two years of living there was enough for me. But after being over here as long any place in God's country would be heaven. I haven't seen anything over here to even begin to compare with the good old U.S.

Write again will you Elly? Hoping all is well with you and the big city.

Sincerely,
Mitch

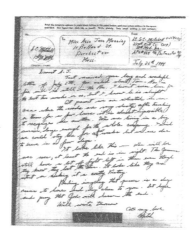

July 26, 1944

Dearest A.J.

Just received your long and wonderful letter of July 6th. You asked about Tom. He is fine and is still in the Bn. I haven't seen him for the last two weeks or so, but I know he is alright.

At present we are situated in an area where the roads are very dusty, after traveling them for a few hours it is almost impossible to recognize one another. We are living in a big mansion, large enough for the whole company. I wish we could stay here for a few weeks but we are due to leave in a few days.

July 26, 1944

It looks like this _____ war will be over soon, at least the end is in sight. The Germans still have a lot of fight left in them even they know they lost the war. It looks like they are intent on making it a costly victory.

Darling everyday that passes is a day nearer to home and a day closer to you. Lets hope and pray that God will hasten the end.

Will write tomorrow.

All my love,
Mitch

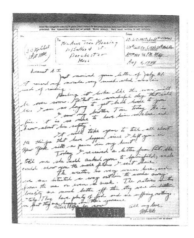

AUG. 6, 1944

Dearest A.J.

Just received your letter of July 21. It raised my morale very much which was in need of raising.

Darling it looks like this war will be over soon. What a wonderful day that will be.. I am so longing to get back home to you. I saw my brother Tom today. He is fine. It is so nice to have him so close and know about his safety.

It will take years to tell all about the things that have happen since I left you in New York, with a pain in my heart.

Today I received a letter from Pat. She told me she had asked you to Springfield, so she could show you the movie films I sent home.

Aug. 6, 1944

The weather is very warm here, and we are situated a way out in the woods away from the sea or even a creek. The natives in the locality are much better off then they were in Southern Italy. They have plenty of food and are suffering nothing, in part they are happy in their ignorance.

Will close for now.

All my love,
Mitch

AUG 27, 1944

Dearest A. J.

Yesterday was a red-letter day for me as I received a lot of
back mail Four letters were from you darling. In all your
letters you asked for a picture of me. Since I have been
overseas I had about four snapshots taken and they weren't
so hot. But I promise at the first opportunity I will send
you one.

Pat told me she had invited you to Springfield to see the
movie film I sent home. A few weeks ago I sent seven more
rolls. I hope they come out. Pat also said that I would
have a lot of explaining to do if you saw them as it seems
a nurse appears in some of the films. I don't think I will
as you know or haven't I told you that since you came into
my life and before no one has made my heart miss a beat
like you did and always will.

Aug 27, 1944

Tom is fine. I see him about once every week. He is a swell fellow. I wish you had met him. It seems you just missed one another in Springfield.

We are still in Italy, although we almost were in on the Southern France deal We were all set to go, then at the last moment our orders were cancelled. The pen can change things very fast.

Although the end of this war is in sight, we still know that there is a war going on. In fact every now and then we get a real reminder. Only last night we had a close reminder.

Finnen is still with us, although he is in another company I see him quite often. I had a long talk with him yesterday. He always asks about you.

Darling I am glad you liked the bracelets and pin. I haven't been anywhere near Rome since the day I bought them. I still have hopes of getting back there for a few days rest.

At present we aren't very busy, but by the time you received this letter I expect we will be very busy.

Well my sweet one I will close with a promise to write soon.

All my love,
Mitch

SEPT. 27, 1944

Dearest A.J.

*Darling please excuse the long delay in writing. Day
after day I have been saying tomorrow. I must find time
to write Anne, then night comes and I am unhappy
with myself for not writing at least a V-mail My sweet
I promise that tomorrow or the day after I will write a
long letter. By the way my cheree you are not doing so well
yourself. I am glad you like the ring. I am still trying to
get a picture of myself to send you.*

*This war should be over now, but those _____ Germans
won't say uncle. Right now the fighting in Italy is as severe
as it has ever been. I hope that it will end before the first
of the year is over. The weather here is due to turn soon
and we aren't looking forward to the rain and mud.*

Everyday that passes is a day nearer to you. Lets hope and pray that, that day isn't to far off.

Will close darling hoping all is well with you.

All my love,
Mitch

OCT 6, 1944

Dearest A.J.,

Just received your letter of Sept 8, and how I would have loved to have been sitting with you against the sea wall What a difference in atmosphere. I am writing this letter in one of the worst storms we have had here this year by candlelight. It is raining, thundering, and lightening, and I expect this tent to go down soon. We are fortunate though—as we have acquired a nice stove, which keeps us warm and dry. I am glad I don't have to go out tonight— my heart goes out to those Infantry soldiers out there in holes filled with water. The mud in these mountains is knee deep. Even in this tent the mud is ankle deep and the stove has been going continually for three days. Enough of my complaints.

Oct 6, 1944

Listen my sweet one what gave you the idea I was coming home with a nurse? Let me get you straight on this matter. I do know a few nurses, but none well enough to take home, nor any that I want to take home. I haven't seen anything in my travels that I want to take home. Since I met you there has been nobody but you. I hope you are straight on the subject You better be or your little ears will get the cutting instead of my big ones. Don't worry about the nurses honey we are seldom very near them, occasionally we are set up near a field hospital, but usually we are quite a few miles in front of them. Even if they were with us there isn't any of them that can get you off my mind

The storm has let up quite a bit and the stove feels real good Really darling at present I don't have any pictures of myself. I did have a few snapshots taken but they weren't so good so I didn't send you any. But I will.

I saw Tom today. He is fine and is in very good health. In fact he is putting on a little weight.

Darling I have but one wish and that is to get back on the other side of the pond to you and the sea wall. How about throwing me a rope.

My sweet I will close this letter, as the wind is coming up again, and the candle is about to blow out.

All my love,
Mitch

NOV. 1944

*With Best Wishes for a Merry Christmas and a Happy
New Year*

Hoping our next will be together.

All my love,

Mitch

NOV. 8, 1944

Dearest A. J.

Darling please excuse my laxity in writing. To this fault I can attribute many things such as climactic conditions, high altitude, rain, mud, cold wind, amount of work, but not my lack of love for you. Anne I can't get home soon enough to be with you. It is going on two years since we parted—a long time to be away from the one you love. My morale is at the lowest it has been since I have been over seas—reason being I felt sure we wouldn't spend another winter in Italy. I had thoughts of being with you for New Years, but right now they look fairly slim.

Today was a red-letter day. I received two letters from you. One dated Sept 20 and the other written from Canada. The latter had me baffled at first, as I couldn't imagine what you were doing in Canada. I was on the point of sharpening my knife to do some ear chopping.

171

In your letter of Sept 20 you asked what I would like for Xmas. Could you wrap yourself up in a neat little package? Really darling there isn't anything I want. My only desire at present is to see this war end and come home to you.

You can send your love and that will be all I will want for this Xmas.

Tom is fine. Although I don't see him very often, as our duties keep us apart, I am always aware of his doings.

Since I last wrote I had three days leave in Rome. It was a changed city since the last time I was there. Now in Rome you wouldn't know there was a war going on only a few hundred miles away. The people are well dressed and from outward appearances don't seem to be lacking in the necessities of life. There are a lot of things which are hard to take and which I cant mention until it is all over, but I imagine we wont want to talk about them then. But I can't feel sorry for these people.

Your sister Irene is certainly giving you and your mother a lot of trouble. She will get over her streak—we all have them. I know I use to give my Mother plenty of gray hairs. How is Elly? Fine I hope. Is she still in New York?

Pat said she hasn't heard from you lately but planned to see you when she was in Boston. She is planning on seeing one of B.C's football games.

I will say good night dear and promise that I will write again tomorrow.

All my love,
  Mitch

Nov. 14, 1944

NOV. 14, 1944

Dearest A.J.

*Just a short note to let you know I love you very much and
to warn you not to make eyes at those ship builders.*

*Darling things are about the same except the weather.
We have already had our second snowfall. The next three
or four months are going to be hard to take. At present
we are situated in a small little town away up in the
mountains. The natives are all very poor and not very
progressive. Occasionally we are able to get into a large
city where one is able to take in an Opera. The Officers
Club is fair, the drinks are terrible, native gin and cognac
but it is better than nothing. I haven't done any drinking
for nearly a year now. Every month we receive a case of
beer and one quart of good whiskey.*

173

Tom is fine, at present he is at a rest camp for four days. I saw him just before he left.

Darling I will close this short note, but will write again tomorrow.

All my love,
Mitch

NOV. 16, 1944

Dearest A.J.

Just a short note before I crawl into my sleeping bag. By the way darling if you go to Washington my sister Rita is there. Her address is 1314 Mass. Ave. She is living with her sister-in-law. I hope you didn't go without seeing her. She has been in Washington since her husband went overseas. I am sure you would enjoy your visit with her.

Please excuse the writing as I am writing this by candlelight sitting on my cot. I wish you were here with me. I am sure it would make this place look like heaven instead of what it is really like.

DEAREST A.J.

We have had our third fall of snow so far, but yesterday it rained most of the day, washing it all away leaving only mud.

Finnen is fine. I saw him the day before yesterday. We talked about you. He says Hello.

Well my sweet I will close this short note and get into my sleeping bag and try to dream of you.

All my love,
Mitch

NOV. 17, 1944

Dearest A.J.

Just received your wonderful letter of Oct 30ᵗʰ. You can show the Postmaster this letter so you can send me those magazines. I would love to have them esp. coming from you.

As yet I haven't taken a picture of myself, but my sweet one the next time I go into town I will have one taken. I haven't been in any town or city of any size for he last two months.

Oh Anne I also wish I were coming home soon. I thought I would be home for Xmas this time last year. Lets both pray and hope that it will be soon. I keep day dreaming what I will do when I get back. Where I will take you and etc. Oh what a sweet pipe.

I have received the Papal blessing for your family but as yet haven't sent it home. What I think I will do is to send

*it to Peg and have her forward it to you. Have three others
to send as I will send them all at once.*

Well my sweet one I will close for now.

*All my love,
Mitch*

NOV. 24, 1944

Dearest A.J.

Enclosed is a pair of rosaries, which were blessed by the Pope. I am also sending you a pair for your Mother.

Yesterday we had a wonderful Thanksgiving dinner, our second one overseas, and I pray and hope our last. This year circumstances were a little better than last, in that we had most of the company present. Last year most of the company ate their dinner in a fox hole. Could it be that next year we partake of the same turkey?—I hope so.

Darling please excuse the writing as it is by candle light on a C ration box, and the hour is late.

The weather has been terrible the last few days, but we are preparing ourselves for worse to come. According to the natives they have some real heavy snowstorms in this locality.

Well my sweet I will close this short note with all my love to you and wishing I were near enough to touch you.

Love,
Mitch

P.S. Will write a note tomorrow

NOV. 26, 1944

Dearest A.J.

Enclosed is a pair of rosaries for your Mother. Like your pair they also were blessed by His Holiness the Pope. I hope she will like them

I just received your letter of Nov. 3 it was wonderful You were wondering how and in what way I have changed. Darling that is hard for me to say. Physically I did lose a little weight, but I am beginning to put a little of it back on. And at present I feel fine. I image y   biggest change, which is also true of almost everyone over here is mentally, but as soon as this is over it wont be hard to revert back to a normal way of living.

Within the next few weeks I expect to have a few days leave in Rome. While I will try to get a snapshot of myself to send to you.

DEAREST A.J.

Darling you also asked how much affection I need and want. Honey a little from you will go a long way.

Right now it is hard to answer that question. But I think I am going to want a lot. How about you?

My sweet I will close for now.

All my love,
Mitch

NOV. 27, 1944

Dearest A.J.

I feel in a writing mood, which is seldom, esp. on a day like this. It is raining which isn't unusual, as it has been raining for days, but it is terribly foggy. Just like in one of those dreary scenes in the movies. But I did have to write a short note to tell you how much I miss you and how much I love you. I just cant get home fast enough, everyday over here drags on so.

The mail situation has been bad the last few weeks and to top it all off we received some outgoing mail back, which had been damaged by fire. I haven't received any mail from you for two weeks now. Darling I so look forward to your letters.

DEAREST A.J.

A few days ago I mailed you a pair of rosaries and another pair for your mother. I hope you received them. I enclosed them in a letter to you.

Well my sweet I hope this short note finds you in the very best of health.

All my love,
Mitch

Dec. 23, 1944

DEC. 23, 1944

Dearest A.J.

Darling I just received your two packages and of all days to get them on my birthday. Thanks a lot for the toilet kit it will certainly come in handy. I would love to be with you today instead of sitting in this old dilapidated Italian building—what a way to spend a birthday. I hope the next one will be with you.

I do think of you so much, esp. during this season when we should be together. Instead we are separated by this terrible war. Right now the news from France isn't so bright, but I am sure that one day we will wake up and this mess will be all over, I have a feeling that it will come when we least expect it. I hope it will be soon.

In your letter of Nov. 22 you were home sick. Now my sweet you better stay well and stop worrying so much and

185

don't knock yourself out working so hard. When I get home I want you in tiptop shape

As yet I haven't had a snapshot taken but I will have one soon (if the weather clears up).

Did you receive the rosaries I sent you and your Mother?

Will close now my dream girl. Write more often. I promise to savor every letter you write.

All my love,
Mitch

Dec. 26, 1944

DEC. 26, 1944

Dearest A.J.

*I was just starting this short note to you when the
company clerk brought me a letter from you. It was
so wonderful to hear from you, to know that you are
thinking about me.*

Since I last wrote I had a four-day leave in Rome.

*Other than the fact that the people are deprived of certain
food commodities and the appearance of American soldiers
one would never believe a savage war was raging in the
country. While in Rome I went to a trotting race and won
$96. I got to the track for the last three races and won
every one of them. I enjoyed the races very much because
it was one place and one time where I almost forgot about
the war.*

Darling it has been a long time since we have been separated. But as you say God is good, he will bring us together soon again.

My sweet I just got another letter from you this one is dated Nov. 22. I will now read it and promise to answer it tomorrow.

For now

All my love,
Mitch

JAN. 1, 1945

Dearest A.J.

Last night was a lonely night, mainly because I wasn't with you. At midnight I had a drink of very good scotch whiskey. I drank to you and that 1945 would be our year that this was would end soon and we would be together again.

This afternoon I was fortunate to be able to attend a New Years football game, which was played in Florence, between the 12'1' Air Corps and the 5'1' Army. Did you read about the game in the paper? It was a beautiful football day. The sun was strong in a bright clear sky, and the wind was brisk without being biting. There were about 15,000 present and the atmosphere was 100 American. It was just like a traditional college game, with bands, cheerleaders and team mascots—the 12ᵗʰ Air Force (bridgebusters) had a long horned steer for a mascot, while the 5ᵗʰ Army (mudbusters) had a mule—who was the cutest thing I ever saw in the

*mule family. He would run across the field butting like
a bull and then kick his hind feet in the air. It was very
exciting and at times you would forget you were in Italy—it
was just like being at a game at home—you would hear loud
good-natured cracks—a few drunks and a fight here and
there. Fifth Army won by a score of 20-0. Although the score
was one sided it still was a close and hard fought game.*

*Between the halves the bands played and floats passed in
review. Ella Logan sang two songs I never heard before:
"Take Me Out to the Old Spaghetti Bowl Game" and
"Straighten Up and Fly Right". I am enclosing a program.*

*My love did you receive the rosaries I sent for you and
your Mother.*

*I saw Tom this morning. He received your Xmas package.
I hope he writes his thanks, according to my folks he is
worse than me when it comes to writing.*

*Finnen wanted to be remembered He is still as witty as
ever. He is a lot of fun to be around.*

*Darling for a New Years promise—I will promise to write
you as often as possible. At times it is very difficult to
write esp. when the war news isn't so good.*

I will close wishing you and your family a very happy 1945.

*All my love,
Mitch*

P.S. I could use the sweater now.

190

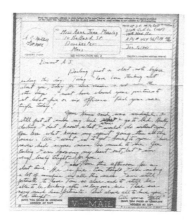

JAN 4, 1945

Dearest A.J.

Darling just a short note before ending this day. Today I have been thinking a lot about you, today for some reason a lot more than other days. I must have showed your picture to at least five or six officers. Did your nose tingle today?

Your Xmas card was wonderful. I still put it under my head when I go to bed. Really darling I don't know what I would do without you. You are what keeps my spirit going thru all this mess. All I want is to get home to you. I have never had anyone mean so much to me. Gee darling I am praying my heart out, but I am very lonely tonight for you.

I saw Tom this afternoon for a short time. He is fine. Even thought I am making a lot of sacrifices in all this mess. I am still fortunate to have Tom so close and to still be able to be kicking after so long over here. There are many much less fortunate. And above all to have you. For tonight.

All yours,
Mitch

JAN. 19, 1945

Dearest A.J.

Darling isn't the war news wonderful, if it keeps up we may be together sooner than I thought a few weeks ago. Oh! It is going to be so exciting to get home and have you in my arms.

The mail at present is very slow. I haven't had a letter from you in two weeks. It will all come in at the same time.

Yesterday I went skiing and last night I could hardly walk. My arms and legs are still sore. I took some movies of the ski run; some to the shots should be very good.

Everytime I went down the run I ended up in a horizontal position.

Jan. 19, 1945

I saw Tom today. He said he was going to write you tonight. I am sure you will like him. He is a fine fellow— of course—he takes after me. He really does look good as he has put on a little weight.

Darling every night before I fall to sleep my thoughts are of you. I feel that soon we will be together again.

Keep praying that it will be soon.

All my love,
Mitch

FEB. 1, 1945

A VALENTINE
from One who Cares

You'll never know how much I care—
How much I think about you—
Words cannot tell you how I feel,
So far way, without You—
But meanwhile, all my thoughts are in
This Valentine I'm sending—
A world of love, and wishes, too,
For happiness unending!

All my love,
Mitch

FEB. 11, 1945

Dearest A.J.

Darling please excuse the long delay in writing. I am always thinking of you, both day and night. Please don't feel that the lapse in my writing is a wavering of my love. If my love for you were measured by letter writing, you would receive a letter a minute.

I have sent you an Easter present. I won't tell you what it is, just let it be a surprise. I hope you will like it.

The war news has been very good the last few days. I really do believe that summer will bring with it the end of this mess.

Darling please excuse the writing, as I am writing on an old return box, which isn't too comfortable.

DEAREST A.J.

The radio news just announced that you have had a bad storm in New England. I hope it doesn't last to long. The weather here has been fine the last few days, but we expect a few more weeks of miserable weather.

Well my sweet until tomorrow.

All my love forever,
Mitch

Feb. 14, 1945

FEB. 14, 1945

Dearest A.J.

Yesterday I received the fruitcake you sent. Thank you darling, it was very good.

The war news is wonderful and it really looks like this mess will be over soon. With the help of God we may be together this summer. It has been a long time—hasn't it my sweet one?

I am anxious to receive a letter from you after you receive the present I sent to you for Easter. I really do hope you like it. Since I last wrote you I had to make a trip to Rome.

I was only in the city for one day as the trip was for official business. I made the trip by train and I still feel worn out. It took seventeen hours one way and you should

197

have seen the coaches we rode on. The compartments were built to accommodate four people and most of the compartments had eight soldiers in them.

Darling I will close now—will write again tomorrow.

All my love,

Mitch

FEB. 21, 1945

Dearest A.J.

Darling please excuse the long delays between my letters. Within the last few days I have received four wonderful letters from you. They did a lot for me, much better than a big juicy steak. For the past two weeks I was on a job which made letter writing impossible. So my dear I will try to redeem myself by writing you a long letter.

Let me start off by telling you how much I miss you, and how I long for the day we are together again. Darling I do love you so. I get a lump in my throat by just looking at your picture. Darling I do want to get home soon. I am so sick of this war, but it looks like the end is in sight—I hope so.

I was so pleased that you and your mother liked the rosaries and the Papal blessing so much.

In one of your letters you mentioned the possibility of my spending the summer at the beach with you—Oh Anne, how wonderful that would be — My sweet it could be anywhere and any season as long as it was with you.

Did Tom write and thank you for the gift you sent him for Xmas? The last time I saw him he said that he was going to write you. He is much worse than I when it comes to writing letters. I know that sounds impossible. I haven't seen Tom for sometime now, but I know he is O.K.

Darling we had so little time together and so much time apart. Please darling don't get impatient, it shouldn't be to long now. It will be fun making up the lost time. We have so many things to do together.

Did you receive my Easter present yet? I hope you like it. Let me know what your folks think of it.

Feb. 21, 1945

In your letter of Jan. 26 you mentioned having attended a wedding in which there was no head or tail to it. What kind of a wedding do you want my sweet? Or should we wait until I get home so you can tell me. It will be much nicer to talk about than to write about.

Darling you don't have to fear about the nurses and WACS over here even if they were Hollywood's best. You are all that I want.

I received your two pictures. They are very good; I have been showing you off to everyone. At present they are in Florence being framed. They are wonderful my sweet thing.

Quite sometime ago I promised to send you a picture of myself. Darling as yet I haven't had one taken, but my sweet the next time I get in to a town I will have one taken. Then you can throw that magnifying glass away.

The mail has been very slow even mail going to the States. I hope this letter travels a little faster than usual because it has been over a week since I have written. Darling if I could tell you why I haven't written. I am sure you would give me a big kiss, instead of a reprimand.

As yet I haven't received the sweater you sent nor your Mother's letter. You know my sweet I should have met your family before I come overseas, and I should have been with you when you met my family. We were very selfish always wanting to be alone—but it was wonderful I will

201

never forget how I felt the night I left you on the train in the Grand Central Station. It was then that I was sure, oh so sure, that I had it bad.

I am glad to hear that you are saving your money. You know my sweet you are going to need a little of that paper to support me after this war is over. I won't need much say about a hundred a week for pin money. But seriously my sweet I don't want you spending a lot of money on clothes when I cant see you in them. Take that fur coat you bought I just picture you walking down the street and all those lucky guys giving you the once over. I want you to save those glad rags for me.

My darling I will close hoping all is well with you and your family.

All my love,
Mitch (or Ves)

FEB. 22, 1945

Dearest A.J.

Just received your letter of Feb. 14th. It was such a nice letter that I had to answer it immediately. Darling I am sorry that I was lax in writing, but the majority of the laxity was due to circumstances, which were uncontrollable.

The weather has been beautiful the last two weeks. Most of the snow has gone, except for isolated spots on the high mountains. According to the radio and your last letter you are still undergoing a very severe winter. It looks as if winter has passed for us. I hope it is the last one that I have to spend on this side of the ocean.

Thank your Mother for praying that I will be home this coming summer. I hope that her prayers will be answered God has been very good to me so far in this war.

DEAREST A.J.

Now my sweet you better be a good girl, if for your penance, if bad,—you lose me. Darling I know you will be good, so I feel sure that I won't be the lamb to be sacrificed.

I received a letter from Pat today; telling me about the flowers you sent my Mother. She said that they were very nice—all spring flowers.

Size said that they were having such terrible weather that the flowers made them think of spring. That was very sweet of you darling.

Darling I miss you so much. Each passing day brings us closer· together. I live for the day that I get into a telephone booth and telephone you. Oh, it will be so nice to hear your voice again.

Have you received the package I sent you? I am so anxious for it to arrive and I hope it is in good condition.

I have been working fairly hard the last two weeks, but I will be able to take it easy for awhile (I hope). I wish I could take it easy with you on the Cape.

Well my dear I will close for now hoping all is well with you.

All my love,
Mitch

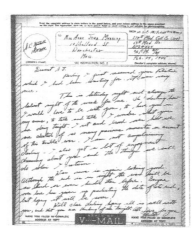

FEB. 24, 1945

Dearest A.J.

Darling I just received your Valentine, which I had been waiting for. It was very nice.

This is Saturday night and always the loneliest night of the week for me. Oh! Darling how I would love to be with you, to have you in my arms, to talk and talk. I wonder what you are doing tonight. I sit and brood over how we are cheated of so many precious moments on account of this terrible war. I am not complaining darling. I also get a lot of enjoyment dreaming about you and the things we will do when I return.

War news is again looking good. Although the end is in sight the war will be as hard or even harder than before. Everyone over here has given up predicting the date of its end, but hoping it will be soon.

Will close darling hoping all is well with you, and that you are thinking of me tonight.

All love for you,
Mitch

MARCH 2, 1945

Dearest A.J.

Just a short note my sweet to let you know that I am thinking of you tonight and love you very much. Oh Anne I do hope and pray that this war will end soon and we will be together.

The weather has been wonderful the last month. The natives claim that it was the warmest Feb. in the last twenty-five years.

Darling as yet I haven't received the sweater you sent. It will come in handy for these cool spring nights.

The war news is still very good I don't see why the Germans continue their useless struggle. I don't see the immediate end of this mess in sight, but I believe it will be this coming spring or summer.

DEAREST A.J.

I saw Tom last night for the first time in the last two weeks. He is fine and is in the best of spirits. I am sure you will like Tom when you meet him. He is very nice—there I go bragging. Finnen is fine—He told me to say hello for him.

Tonight is very foggy out you can't see your hand in front of you.

We would rather have nights like that rather than with a full moon—at certain times anyways.

Last night I saw my first movie in a few weeks. It was so terrible that I can't remember the name. Deanna Durbin played the leading role—she was a Senator's daughter. There wasn't one good song in the whole show. She had better make a new show real soon.

Darling I will close this short note and get into my sleeping bag where I will say good night to you and pick you up in my dreams.

Hoping all is well with you.

All my love,
Mitch

MARCH 4, 1945

Dearest Darling,

This afternoon I received the two pictures of you, which I had framed in Florence. They are wonderful I had them cut out and mounted on a white background. I have been showing them to everyone that comes within a hundred yards of me. Darling it will be wonderful when I can show you off in person. The chaplain just came in—he likes the same pose that I do. They have all been asking me why a handsome thing like you would have anything to do with a _____ _____ guy like me. They are really riding me, but my sweet I know I have something precious when I have you.

I am sure the package you sent me, in which you left off the APO#, will arrive O.K. At New York the postmaster has the APO# of every outfit over seas. I will be looking forward to contents of the package—you are sweet.

DEAREST A.J.

Darling I know I have been very lax in writing and I know that you have every right to be dubious about receiving an avalanche of mail But really my sweet thing at times it is hard to write both for physical as well as mental reasons. But I want you to know that my love for you cannot be weighted by the number of letters I write. You are on my mind continually.

Now my sweet about this driver that is bringing you gardenias. I hope he is a married man with about fifteen children, and is fat, and about fifty years old, no teeth, baldhead, and all that stuff. Darling I know you are liked so by the people you come in contact with that they want to be liked by you.

My sweet I hope this letter finds you in as good health as I am.

All my love,
"Mitch"

MARCH 10, 1945

Dearest A.J.

Just a short note before going to bed. Darling I have been thinking of you, more than usual, today—maybe because I am so elated about the war news in this theater. The crossing of the Rhine and the battle on the west bank of the Rhine. The news is so good that I have been dreaming of coming home to you. I let my thoughts run wild—it was wonderful

I received a letter from you yesterday. Your letters do so much for me, and you have been so good in your correspondence lately. I will try to do more writing in the future.

The weather is fine here at present—real nice spring weather. We have been very fortunate in having such fine weather, although we certainly did get our share of bad weather.

You must be having a hard time trying not to resist those new spring outfits. I don't have any civilian clothes that I can wear when I get out of the Army. Just this morning, Sgt

Lynch, our 1ˢᵗ Sgt, and I were talking about clothes, what type suits we liked . We had a few old Esquire magazines to look over. It was fun thinking about civilian life. Now my sweet don't buy to many of those dazzling spring outfits—at least until I get home.

For the last few days I have had a miserable head cold which I don't seem to be able to shake off.

As yet my sweet I haven't had a picture taken, but this coming week I will have one taken as I expect to go into Florence for a day.

I am anxious to hear how you liked the last package I sent you.

Everyone I showed it to here liked it very much.

Will close for now.

With all my love

Completely yours,
Mitch

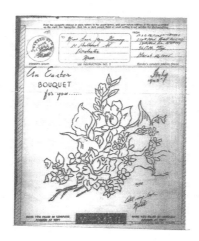

MARCH 12, 1945

AN EASTER BOUQUET

FOR YOU......

ITALY 1945

All my love,
Mitch

MARCH 13, 1945

Dearest A.J.

No letter from you today. I am not complaining because
you have been good lately. But I do love to get your letters
Anne. They mean so much to me.

As yet my sweet I haven't received your package. It should
be here soon. I hope you have received the package I sent
you. You should be receiving it about now. If you don't
like it my sweet say so and I will have another one made.
I liked it very much in fact the more I looked at it the
better I liked it If you haven't received it you don't know
what I am talking about, but I wanted it to be a surprise
to you, so I wont say what it is.

In one of your letters you asked what plans I have when I
get home. My sweet all my plans are surrounded around
you. I don't know what I am going to do. Can you get me
a job selling newspapers? I am so undecided about going

214

March 13, 1945

back with Hills Brothers. It has been almost five years since the Army pulled me into this present environment.

I was thinking of going back to school to brush up a little, but I have given that up. Yes my darling I would like you to tell me of your dreams, hopes and wishes.

I am enclosing a few cartoons which one of the EMS gave me. What do you think of them? I don't think things have gone that far.

The war news is still very good, but my sweet we are at such a stage that we can't get over optimistic. When the end does come it will take sometime to really believe it.

In on of your letters you asked me to send you some movie film. At present I have only one roll of colored film, which I have been saving waiting to get some good, shots. Peg has been having a lot of trouble lately finding film. But I will send you some, as I believe Peg has some film in the mail If you can find some in Boston I would appreciate it. The only type that will fit my camera is 8mm and not 8mm magazine fed I know it is almost impossible to find.

Anne I will close for tonight (it is now early morning about 2 minutes after twelve) hoping to find you in my dreams. My sweet one I do love you oh so much.

All yours,
"Mitch"

MARCH 22, 1945

Dearest A.J.

*I have a complaint to offer to you my sweet—no mail
from you in the last week. As yet the mail hasn't come
in for today but it should be here within a half-hour—I
hope there is a letter from you. Are you giving me some of
my own medicine? I know that I deserve it*

*Oh Anne I am thinking of you constantly. Everyday
that passes is a day closer to you. The war news is very
good and at present even I am getting optimistic. I really
believe that it will be over within a few months.*

*Yesterday I received the two sweaters and two pair of wool
socks. They were very nice, and will be useful as the nights
will be cool thru-out the spring weather.*

*I had some photographs taken, but it will be a week or
so before I will be able to pick them up. In the interim I*

am enclosing a snapshot which was taken on Xmas day. It was taken by one of the EM in the company and I was unaware of its being taken. The little children are from an orphanage in the town where we were located. We had a party for them and the men made each one a package of goodies from the packages they received from home.

The mail just came in, and no letter from the girl I love. Now my sweet little darling you sit down and write me a letter. And tell me how much you miss me, how you want me home "tout suite," how much you love me—tell me all the things I like to hear.

You should have received the painting by now. I hope it was an enjoyable surprise. If you don't like it I will have another one made from one of the last two photographs you sent.

Hoping all is well with you darling, will write again tomorrow.

All my love,
Mitch

MARCH 28, 1945

Dearest A.J.

Just received your letter of March 19th. It was the first letter from you in over a week. I was a little worried thinking you were sick. As yet I haven't received your Mother's letter. I will answer it immediately. It could have been sent on a slow ship. Often times we are apt to receive mail dated over a month and a half at the time we receive it.

March 28, 1945

Your letter was wonderful. Oh! Anne it did so much for me. The men know that they can ask for almost anything on the days that I receive a letter from you. I can tell I have a letter from you before it gets into my hands because the mail clerk has a big smile when he comes up to me.

The war news is wonderful It should be over soon. It would be a great gift from God if it would end before Easter Sunday.

In the first paragraph of your letter you asked how long it would he before I get home.

Darling I don't want to make any promises but it should be this summer. An officer in the company Lt. Clark is going home in a few days. When he gets home he will have forty-five days in the States and then he starts back. He is going home under very unfavorable conditions as his wife has been confined in the State Hospital with TB and isn't doing to well I have given him your address, and he has promised to telephone you from Baltimore.

I am getting that spring feeling also and long more and more to he with you. Do you ever find me in your dreams? Most every night when fall off to sleep I live over the times we were together—the things we did—what we said and the many things we should have said.

By the time you receive this letter you should have received your painting. I am anxious to know how you like it.

In your letter you mentioned some snapshots that you enclosed in one of your letters—my sweet one, as yet I haven't received that letter. It may come in—in a few days. I have been unable to get into town to pick up my photographs. I hope that they are good

I have wished and prayed that I would be with you this Easter, but as the good books tells us—we must suffer on this earth. I hope you receive my flowers in time for Easter, with the card, which I had our mail clerk make. I was going to send an orchid, but changed my mind when in one of your letters you mentioned that gardenias were your favorite flowers.

Darling I would love to help you put on some weight Maybe we could help each other as I have a lot of weight to put on, and could think of no better way of putting it on. Oh my sweet how I miss you. All my prayers are to get home in one piece to you. Tom is fine, although I haven't seen him in the last two weeks I do get a report about him every now and then.

Finnen is still as witty as ever and has been in very good spirits. Since the change in the war everyone is in very high spirits and all looking forward to an early end I see Finnen almost everyday as our company is very close to his.

Anne keep your spirits up and pray that this will be over soon. I am positive that we are now on the downhill slope of that big mountain.

Give my best wishes to your family and keep in mind that I love you very much.

All yours,
"Mitch"

Dearest A.J.

Today was a red letter day for me. I received two letters (wonderful letters) and a package from you. The package contained a wonderful bottle, which is at present being admired by two other officers. I don't know how long it will be before the top will come off. The two officers (Davis & Fish) are pleading with me to open it up. I think I have teased them enough so here goes. It is real good.

Your letters were dated March 23rd and March 29th. In your letter of March 29th a snap-shot of you was enclosed It was very good. Are those gloves you are wearing the gloves I sent you?

I am glad to see you and buying war bonds. As you say it may come in handy in about ten years. In a letter from home I received a statement from my bank and my sweet I am doing much better than I had anticipated But what gets me mad is that I should be drawing Captain's pay. My promotion went in about seven months ago, but it was turned down because of a change in T/O (table of organization). Don't get me wrong darling I still consider myself very fortunate in comparison to others.

Just had another drink the second (both of them for you my sweet). Both Davis & Fish say thanks for your thoughtfulness.

Darling I am more than pleased that you like your painting so much. I do like to please you and always hope to make you happy.

As yet I didn't get into Florence to pick up those photographs I had taken and the way things look I wont be able to get into Florence this coming week. But I will try to have someone pick them up for me.

April 8, 1945

Did you receive my flowers on time for Easter? I hope it wasn't like last year, and they arrive a few weeks later. This Easter was spent high up in the mountains and the weather was wonderful We had a beautiful High Mass and the choir was excellent The altar was decorated with numerous types of flowers, Easter Lilies dominating all the others. The Mass really made us feel that it was Easter and all was well Oh yes I wore a new hat. I hope you had a pleasant Easter and am anxious to receive the snapshots you took

Oh! Anne I am praying for this war to end and to get home to you. The way it looks now Hitler is going to fight until the last German. I can't understand how a few men can have such control over a country when the majority know that they are fighting for a lost cause. Such useless loss of life and limb. The Germans were supposed to be a smart race but individually they are like horses, they must be lead They must have someone to follow. Why they picked Hitler, that (fill in anything as long as it is real bad) is beyond me.

When you receive this letter we should be working hard Remember my sweet that I am always thinking of you and that you have all my love.

Yours,
Mitch

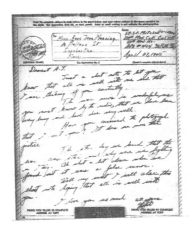

APRIL 27, 1945

Dearest A.J.

Just a short note to let you know that all is well with me and that I am thinking of you constantly.

The war news is wonderful, as you must know by the radio, that we have been very busy and have done very well.

Have you received the photograph that I sent you? It does me more than justice.

The other day we heard that the war was over and why were we fighting in Italy. Oh what a let down when we found out it was a false rumor.

Well my sweet I will close this short note hoping that all is well with you.

I love you so much.

All yours,
Mitch

MAY 4, 1945

Dearest A.J.

Just a short note to let you know that all is well and that I am thinking of you and longing to be with you.

Isn't the news of the surrender of the German armies wonderful? You must have done a lot of celebrating back home. It is strange, but over here there was no celebrating at all. Of course every soldier is very happy and in the very good spirits, but everyone seems to be of the opinion that the time to celebrate is when we get back home to the ones we love.

The Po valley was very beautiful but as you know we came thru it very fast and these Alps are very cold. Right at present I am very cold and in need of a shave.

DEAREST A.J.

I could have taken a minute of history making movie shots of German prisoners (thousands of them), of a fascist executor, and many others but I didn't have my camera with me for fear of losing or breaking it. And when we are working it is hard to get in the mood of taking pictures.

It should all be over soon my love.

Completely yours,
Mitch

MAY 11, 1945

Dearest A.J.

Darling this is the first opportunity I had to write you since the wonderful defeat and surrender of the German Army. They were really beaten and out maneuvered.

I have so much to tell you that I don't know where to begin. I wish I could take off right now so I could tell it to you in person. My name was in to go home this month, but since the end of hostilities all temporary duty to the U.S. has been canceled Everyone is now figuring out their points to get out of the Army. I have between 105-110, which is fairly high, and my possibilities of getting out look good.

During this last drive we had many close calls and there were a few nights that I will never forget The Bn. Was very lucky not one man was lost The first few days were very rough, but then prisoners started to roll in by the thousands. Oh! It was wonderful to see. We all knew that the end was in store a week before it was announced

When it did come there was very little celebrating. Did the people at home do much in the way of celebrating? Our greatest thrill will be landing in the good old U.S.A. where our loved ones are.

At present we are located at Cortina d'Ampeuo in the Italian Alps. It is very beautiful I don't think I have ever seen such scenery in all my travels, Oh! How I wish I could enjoy it with you. It may be soon now. The mountains all around are snow capped and the valley and low hills are green-green and just covered with flowers.

We are located in a beautiful big villa over looking the town. We have running water, both town and Army telephones all over the house.

This town was a big German hospital center and we are now starting to take care of them administratively. The total of patients, help and staff is over 10,000. So you can imagine the work that is involved and only two officers and 60 men are in the company at present. We have seventy-five buildings to guard.

The situation here is strange as Germans partisans, and Americans are still walking around all armed to the teeth. It will take a few days to get things running smoothly.

My sweet I will close this letter as I have been interrupted so many times.

Hoping to be one of the lucky ones and home soon to you.

All my love,
Mitch

May 20, 1945

MAY 20, 1945

Dearest A.J.

*Please excuse the delay in writing. For the last five days
I have been away from the company traveling all over
Northern Italy on Company, Bn., Corps, and Army
business. All this business is in connection with German
hospitals, which are in Northern Italy up to the Austrian
boarder. I am so tired of riding that the only ride I would
take right now would be home. Everything is so scattered,
that it will be a few weeks before things settle down to
some sort of organization. A lot of work is involved in
disarming and taking in the Germans. In some towns
German M.P.s (military police) are still doing traffic duty.
It is strange to see Germans walking around, driving their
own vehicles in convoy to the prison camps.*

*It is wonderful to have the fighting over with; I still can't
believe it.*

Little did I dream that one day I would be in a position to write a pass, or tell a German that he could go here and he couldn't go their, that he would do this and not that When in such a position I wonder how they would treat us if they were in our position. From what they have done all over Europe I am sure that we wouldn't be treated as well as we treat them.

Oh Anne how I long to get home. As yet we don't know what is going to happen. It will be a few weeks before things get settled and we will know where we stand I am going to do all in my power to get an early boat home.

I received your second package, which was very welcomed. It was very good fluid. By the way, did you receive my photo?

I have bought a lot of nik-nacs, which I sent home—some are for us. Tomorrow I am sending you a package.

Will close with all my love.

Completely yours my love,
Mitch

June 1, 1945

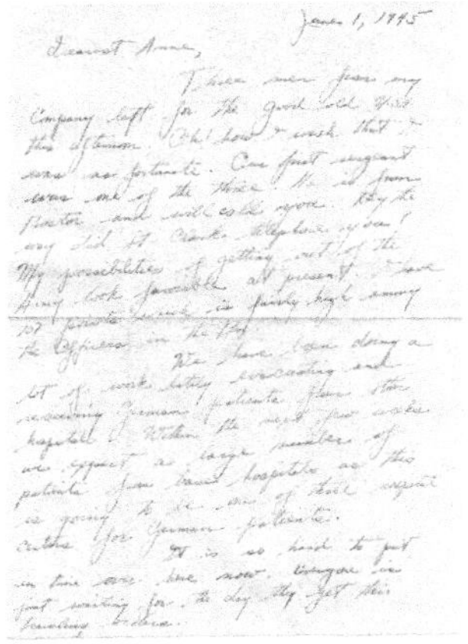

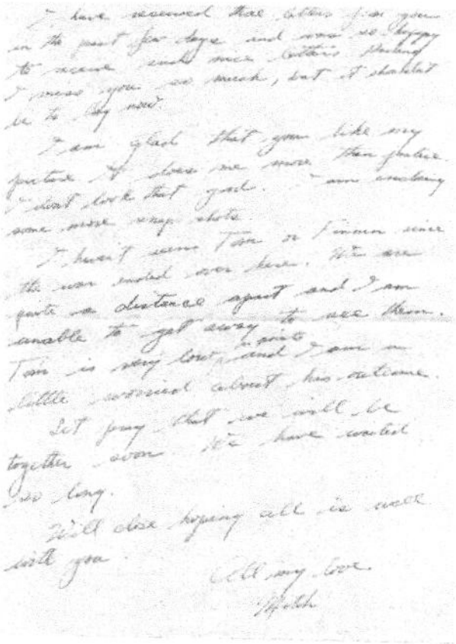

JUNE 1, 1945

Dearest Anne,

Three men from my company left for the good old U.S.A. this afternoon. Oh! How I wish that I was as fortunate. Our first sergeant was on of the three. He is from Boston and will call you. By the way did Lt. Clark telephone you? My possibilities of getting out of the Army look favorable at present. I have 107 points, which is fairly high among the officers in the Bn.

We have been doing a lot of work lately evacuating and receiving German patients from other hospitals. Within the next few weeks we expect a large number of patients from bas hospitals as this is going to be one of three hospital centers for German patients.

It is so hard to put in time over here now. Everyone is just waiting for the day they get their traveling orders.

DEAREST A.J.

I have received three letters from you in the past few days and was so happy to receive such nice letters. Darling I miss you so much, but it shouldn't be to long now.

I am glad that you like my picture. It does me more than justice. I don't look that good. I am enclosing some more snap shots.

I haven't seen Tom or Finnen since the war ended over here. We are quite a distance apart and I am unable to get away to see them. Tom is very low on points and I am a little worried about his outcome.

Lets pray that we will be together soon. We have waited so long.

Will close hoping all is well with you.

All my love,
Mitch

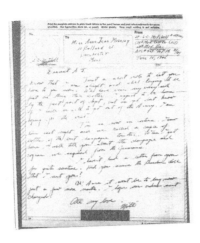

June 18, 1945

JUNE 18, 1945

Dearest A.J.

Just a short note to let you know that I am all right and still longing to be home to you soon. We have been very busy with just one thing than another. I expect to be home by the first part of Sept., but as yet don't know if I will be able to get out of the Army. I am hoping for the best.

Tom is now in Corlina. I saw him last night and we killed a couple of bottles of the best champagne together. When I get home I will tell you about the champagne and cognac we acquired from the Germans.

I haven't had a letter from you for quite sometime. Did you receive the Dresden doll that I sent you?

Oh! Anne it won't be too long now, just a few more months. I hope our orders aren't changed.

All my love,
Mitch

JULY 15, 1945

Dearest A.J.

Please excuse the long delay in writing. I just couldn't apply myself to write. I don't know whether it is the heat or the anticipation of going home. Finally the fear of you ringing my neck when I do get home and my desire to be in your good graces has brought forth this letter. I really am ashamed of myself for not writing sooner and more

*often both to you and home, esp. when I know how much
you look forward to receive my letters.*

*I have been transferred from the 379th to the 38th Evac
Hospital, which is located just outside of Florence. We are
in a Redeployment Area and are classified as a class IV unit
which means going to the States and disband All the Enlisted
men in this unit will be civilian soon after reaching the
States but as yet I don't know the status of the Officers. At
present my possibilities of getting a discharge after returning
home looks very favorable as I have 106 points.*

*The 379th is classified as a class II B unit which will go to
the Pacific by way of the States. I was sorry to leave the Co.
in a way but glad in another. Ever since I got my commission
I was with this Company and have become very attached
to it. But all the high point men have been transferred out
which leaves only about 25% of the original company —
men with under 85 points and I wouldn't like the idea of
going to the States and spend 30 days on furlough and then
get on a boat to the Pacific. I feel that I have done my part
and see no reason for going to the Pacific. If for military
reasons it was necessary then I would feel different about it.*

*Tom is fine. At present he is located at Lake Garda in
Northern Italy. His Co. is classified as a class II C unit
which will go to the States and will be in reserve. That is
they will go to the Pacific if needed.*

*We are now just waiting for a boat. The way it looks now
we wont leave this area until the middle of August, but we
should be in the States the first part of Sept. Oh! happy day.*

DEAREST A.J.

You never mentioned receiving the Dresden doll I sent you. I hope you received it as I meant it for your birthday present.

Oh it is going to be so wonderful to get home again and see you. I hope to get my discharge, but if I don't I will have the first month home free. As soon as I can get to a telephone I will call you.

Don't have anything planned for the whole month of Sept. I expect to end up at Camp Devins from there I will call you.

We will meet in Boston—I will meet your family, then we both will take off for Springfield—stay a few days and from there we can make our plans together.

Will close now my sweet one.

All my love,
Mitch

P.S. Don't write after receiving this letter.

Nov. 20, 1946

My darling Wife,

I thought it would be proper and nice for me to be the sender of the first letter to you in our new home.

What memories are running thru my mind—Of the places where I use to be, and how far away you were when writing to you and how close you are now. This being my first letter to you since our marriage seems very strange esp. after leaving you this morning, in fact after just talking to you on the telephone about a chair for our home.

I wish so much for you and me. I hope that God will be good to us and protect and bless our home. I desire your happiness so much.

So my darling I wish you all the best in our new home.

Your loving,
Husband

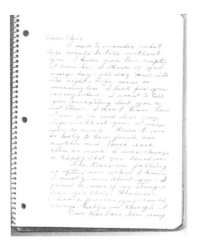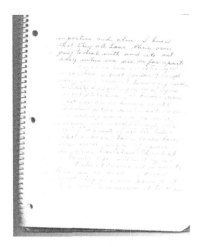

Dear Chris,

I used to wonder what life would be like without you. I know now how empty it can be. I think of you every day— all day and into the night. Life seems so meaningless. I look for you everywhere. I want to tell you everything but you're not there. I don't know how I can go on and live my life without you. I miss you so much. Weren't we lucky to have found one another and loved each other so much. I was always so happy that you loved me.

The tears are falling so often now when I know I must go on without you. I gained so much of my strength from you Chris. Whenever I had a problem you could always help me through it.

Nov. 20, 1946

Our kids have been very supportive and close. I know that they all have their own grief to deal with and it's not easy when we are so far apart.

I was in denial after you died Chris. I just couldn't accept that you weren't here anymore. I talked about you as if you were still here. I know now that you are in heaven with God our Father and that you are looking down on us and helping us work through our grief. I think of all the times I should have, could have, been more aware of your physical limitations. Oh, what a lonely life without you.

Folks at church are so sweet. They are so kind. I know that they feel my pain so it is a warm environment to be in.

Glamour shot of A.J. before the war

Mitch after the war in Cortina d'ampezzo in the Italian Alps.

CITATION

BRONZE STAR MEDAL

SYLVESTER C. MITCHELL, (01542007), First Lieutenant,
Medical Administrative Corps, United States Army. For
meritorious services in support of combat operations
from 10 September 1944 to 2 May 1945, in Italy. Operating an ambulance control point, First Lieutenant MITCHELL
rendered praiseworthy service in the prompt and efficient
evacuation of wounded men. Displaying keen foresight
and resourcefulness, he made a sound and equitable distribution of casualties among the hospitals, insuring
the most effective treatment of critical surgical cases.
The initiative and untiring devotion to duty of First
Lieutenant MITCHELL are exemplary of the finest traditions of the Medical Department of the United States
Army. Entered military service from Springfield, Massachusetts.

The Bronze Star Medal Citation for Mitch at the end of the war

A.J. outside her home at 10 Bullard St., Dorchester, MA.

Mitch somewhere in Italy giving out gifts to Italian children.

Mitch and A.J. just after their wedding with Elly and Tom.

A.J. dancing with
Mitch at the wedding

Mitch and A.J. on their way
to their honeymoon

Mitch and A.J. on a date.

Pregnant A.J. in their first apartment.

Mitch and A.J. vacationing on Lake Winnipesauke, NH.

Mitch and A.J. at the annual Mitchell family reunion on Lake Winnipesauke

The Mitchell annual family reunion has been held since 1982.

Mitch and A.J. celebrating their 50th anniversary.

"Gramps" and "Nana" with five of their seven grandchildren, Kate, Philip, Anna, Kathleen and Grace. (Richard and Christopher born later.)

Mitch and A.J. with their children Kevin, Brian, Jeanne and Chris.

Mitch and A.J. married 53 years.

About the Author

Chris Mitchell has served as the Middle East Bureau Chief for CBN News since arriving in Israel in August 2000 with his wife Elizabeth and children Philip, Kathleen, and Grace. He is the author of Dateline Jerusalem, Destination Jerusalem and ISIS, Iran and Israel. He also serves as the host and Executive Producer of Jerusalem Dateline, a weekly TV program from Israel seen worldwide on numerous networks, including Daystar and GOD TV. Dearest A.J. is his tribute along with brothers Kevin and Brian and sister Jeanne to honor the memory and legacy of their beloved Mom and Dad—Mitch and A.J.

Made in the USA
Coppell, TX
14 February 2022

73584999R00138